The Good Times Songbook

160 SONGS FOR INFORMAL SINGING

James Leisy

ABINGDON PRESS   *Nashville, Tennessee*

SINGER'S EDITION

THE GOOD TIMES SONGBOOK

Copyright © 1974 by Abingdon Press

Vocal and piano arrangements, unless otherwise credited: © 1974 by James Leisy Music.
Translation, compilation, alteration, and adaptation of words and music in all songs: ©
1974 by James Leisy Music. "Hey Lollee," original words by James Leisy: © 1966, 1974
by James Leisy Music. "New River Train," original words by James Leisy: © 1963 by James
Leisy Music. "Tell Me Why" by James Leisy: © 1956 by TM Music. Adaptations with
original words and/or music in "Ain't It a Shame," "A Bicycle Built for Two," "The
Crawdad Song," "Do Lord," "Everybody Loves Saturday Night," "He's Got the Whole World
in His Hands," "I've Been Workin' on the Railroad," "Jacob's Ladder," "Kum Ba Ya," "Now
We'll Make the Rafters Ring," "Oh, Mary, Don't You Weep,' "Paper of Pins," "Shenandoah,"
"Streets of Laredo": © 1974 by James Leisy Music, 10 Davis Drive, Belmont, California,
94002.

I am indebted to Hawthorn Books, Inc., publishers of my earlier book, *The Folk Song
Abecedary,* for permission to reprint some material which appeared in that volume.

ISBN 0-687-15574-6

MANUFACTURED BY THE PARTHENON PRESS, AT
NASHVILLE, TENNESSEE, UNITED STATES OF AMERICA

Preface

The Good Times Songbook is designed to make group singing easier for those of us who can't possibly remember all the songs, words, and tunes we would like to sing. The songs in these pages are ones that have proved to be successful in a wide variety of informal singing situations. You'll find healthy helpings of spirituals, rhythmic gospel songs, swinging folk songs, nostalgic popular songs, Christmas carols, favorite hymns, cumulative songs, rounds, and so on.

All the songs are pitched in comfortable ranges for the average voice, and cues are provided for the adventurers who would like to add an occasional touch of harmonic, rhythmic, or percussive color.

Whether you are singing with a group of three or four around a living-room piano, two dozen folks around a campfire to the accompaniment of strumming guitars, or a hundred or more in a school or church or club auditorium, you should find more than enough variety to keep you occupied entertainingly for as long as you wish.

Available separately is an edition of *The Good Times Songbook* designed for song leaders and accompanists. This includes vocal scores, accompaniment scores for keyboard and fretted string instruments, detailed performance and program suggestions, special arrangement ideas, additional lyrics, and indexes.

Contents

Ain't It a Shame	7
All God's Children Got Shoes	8
Alouette	9
Amazing Grace	10
America	11
America, the Beautiful	12
Angels, from the Realms of Glory	13
Au Clair de la Lune	14
Auld Lang Syne	15
The Battle Hymn of the Republic	16
A Bicycle Built for Two	17
Bill Bailey	18
Blow the Man Down	18
Buffalo Gals	20
Clementine	21
Come and Go with Me	22
Come, Follow	22
The Crawdad Song	23
Dear Lord and Father of Mankind	24
Deck the Halls with Boughs of Holly	25
Do, Lord, Remember Me	26
Down by the Riverside	26
Down in the Valley	28
The Doxology	29
Every Time I Feel the Spirit	30
Everybody Loves Saturday Night	31
Ezekiel Saw the Wheel	32
Fairest Lord Jesus	33
The First Nowell	34
For the Beauty of the Earth	35
The Four Marys	36
The Fox	36
Frère Jacques	38
Froggie Went A-Courting	38
Go Down, Moses	40
Go Tell Aunt Rhody	40
Go, Tell It on the Mountain	41
God Rest You Merry, Gentlemen	42
Goin' Down the Road Feeling Bad	43
Good King Wenceslas	44
Good News	45
The Gospel Train	46
The Great Meat Pie	47
Green Grow the Lilacs	48
Green Grow the Rushes	49
Greensleeves	52
The Gypsy Rover	53
Hallelujah	54
Hark! the Herald Angels Sing	54
Heaven Is So High	55
Here We Come A-wassailing	56
He's Got the Whole World in His Hands	57
Hey Ho! Nobody Home	58
Hey Lollee	58
The Hokey Pokey	59
Holy, Holy, Holy	60
I Am a Pilgrim	61
I Couldn't Hear Nobody Pray	62
I Heard the Bells on Christmas Day	62
I Know Where I'm Going	63
I Love the Mountains	64
I Saw Three Ships	65
I'm Gonna Sing When the Spirit Says Sing	66
I'm on My Way	66
In the Pines	68
It Came upon the Midnight Clear	69
I've Been Workin' on the Railroad	70
Jacob's Ladder	72
Jingle Bells	73
Johnny, I Hardly Knew You	74
Joshua Fought the Battle of Jericho	75
Joy to the World	76
Just a Closer Walk with Thee	77
The Keeper Would A-Hunting Go	78

Kookaburra	79	Scotland's Burning	118
Kum Ba Ya	79	The Seven Joys of Mary	118
Let Me Fly	80	She'll Be Coming 'Round the	
Let My Little Light Shine	80	Mountain	120
Little Black Train Is A-comin'	82	Shenandoah	121
Lolly Too Dum	84	The Sidewalks of New York	122
Lonesome Road	85	Silent Night	122
Lonesome Valley	86	Sing Your Way Home	124
Mary and Martha	86	Sinner Man	125
Michael, Row the Boat Ashore	87	Sipping Cider Through a Straw	126
My Faith Looks up to Thee	88	Six Little Ducks	127
My Gal Sal	89	The Sloop John B.	128
My Home's Across the Smoky		Soldier, Soldier, Will You Marry Me?	129
Mountains	90	Standing in the Need of Prayer	130
New River Train	91	The Star-Spangled Banner	131
Nine Hundred Miles	92	Steal Away	132
Nine Men Slept in a		Stodola Pumpa	133
Boardinghouse Bed	93	The Streets of Laredo	134
Nobody Knows the Trouble I've Seen	94	Sur le Pont d'Avignon	135
Now the Day Is Over	95	Sweetly Sings the Donkey	135
Now We'll Make the Rafters Ring	95	Swing Low, Sweet Chariot	136
O Christmas Tree	96	Taps	137
O Come, All Ye Faithful	97	Tell Me Why	138
O Little Town of Bethlehem	98	Ten Green Bottles	139
Oh, Dear, What Can the Matter Be?	99	There Was an Old Woman	140
Oh, How Lovely Is the Evening	100	There's a Song in the Air	142
Oh, Mary, Don't You Weep	100	This Old Man	143
Oh, Mister Moon	101	This Train	144
Oh, No, John	102	Three Blind Mice	145
Oh, Won't You Sit Down?	103	Tom Dooley	146
The Old Ark's A-Moverin'	104	Trampin'	147
On the First Thanksgiving Day	105	Tumbalalaika	148
On Top of Old Smoky	106	The Twelve Days of Christmas	148
Once There Were Three Fishermen	107	Wanderin'	150
One More River to Cross	108	The Water Is Wide	151
Over the River and Through		We Three Kings of Orient Are	152
the Woods	109	We Wish You a Merry Christmas	153
Paper of Pins	110	What Child Is This?	154
Pick a Bale of Cotton	111	When Johnny Comes	
A Poor Wayfaring Stranger	112	Marching Home	155
Putting on the Style	112	When the Saints Go	
The Riddle Song	114	Marching In	156
Rise and Shine	115	White Coral Bells	157
The Rock Island Line	116	Why Shouldn't My Goose?	158
Roll, Jordan, Roll	117	Worried Man Blues	158
Row, Row, Row Your Boat	117	Zum Gali Gali	160

1
Ain't It a Shame?

Additional lyrics by J.F.L.

American Folk Song
Adapted by J.F.L.

Moderately fast

Continue, as above:

2. Ain't it a shame to have to work on Sunday?
   Ain't it a shame? (Ain't it a shame?)
   Ain't it a shame to have to work on Sunday?
   Ain't it a shame? (Ain't it a shame?)
   Ain't it a shame to have to work on Sunday?
   When you got Monday, Tuesday, Wednesday,
   Oh, you got Thursday, Friday, Saturday,
   Ain't it a shame?

3. Ain't it a shame to lie around on Sunday?

4. Ain't it a shame to stand in line on Sunday?

5. Ain't it a shame to eat chicken on Sunday?

6. Ain't it a shame to kiss the girls on Sunday?

7. Ain't it a shame to sing this song on Sunday?

8. Ain't it a shame to say ain't on Sunday?

7

2
All God's Children Got Shoes

American Negro Spiritual

Lightly

1. I got a shoe,   you got   a shoe,   All God's chil-dren got   shoes.

When I get to heav-en, gon-na   put on   my shoes, I'm gon-na   tramp all   o-ver God's

heav-en.___   Heav-en,___   heav-en.___

Ev-ery-bod-y talk-in' 'bout   heav-en ain't a-go-in' there,   Heav-en,___

heav-en,___   Gon-na tramp all   o-ver God's   heav-en.___

2. I got a robe, you got a robe,
   All God's children got a robe;
   When I get to heaven, gonna put on my robe,
   I'm gonna shout all over God's heaven.
   Heaven, heaven;
   Everybody talkin' 'bout heaven, ain't a-goin' there;
   Heaven, heaven; Gonna tramp all over God's heaven.

Continue, as above:

3. I got a harp, you got a harp.
   Gonna play all over God's heaven.

4. I got a crown, you got a crown.
   Gonna sing all over God's heaven.

5. I got-a wings, you got-a wings.
   Gonna fly all over God's heaven.

3
Alouette

French-Canadian Folk Song

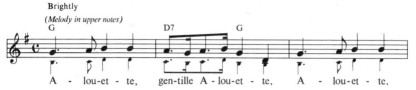

2. Alouette, gentille Alouette,
   Alouette, je te plumerai.
   Je te plumerai le bec,
   Je te plumerai le bec.
   Et le bec, et le bec,
   Et la tête, et la tête,
   Oh-h-h-h

3. Alouette, gentille Alouette,
   Alouette, je te plumerai.
   Je te plumerai le nez,
   Je te plumerai le nez.
   Et le nez, et le nez,
   Et la tête, et la tête,
   Et le bec, et le bec,
   Oh-h-h-h

Continue, as above:

4. Le dos

5. Les pieds

6. Les pattes

7. Le cou

9

4
Amazing Grace

John Newton   *Traditional, American*

Moderately slow

A - maz - ing grace, how sweet the

sound, That saved a wretch like me! I

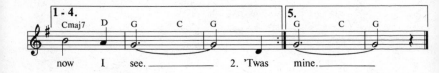

once was lost, but now am found, Was blind, but

now I see. 2. 'Twas mine.

2. 'Twas grace that taught my heart to fear,
   And grace my fears relieved;
   How precious did that grace appear
   The hour I first believed!

3. Through many dangers, toils, and snares,
   I have already come;
   'Tis grace has brought me safe thus far,
   And grace will lead me home.

4. The Lord has promised good to me,
   His word my hope secures;
   He will my shield and portion be
   As long as life endures.

5. The earth shall soon dissolve like snow;
   The sun forbear to shine;
   But God, who called me here below,
   Will be forever mine.

5

America

Samuel Francis Smith

Traditional, European

Moderately slow

1. My coun - try, 'tis of thee, Sweet land of lib - er - ty,

Of thee I sing; Land where my fa - thers died, Land of the

pil - grims' pride, From ev - ery moun - tain-side Let free-dom ring!

2. My native country, thee,
   Land of the noble free;
   Thy name I love:
   I love thy rocks and rills,
   Thy woods and templed hills;
   My heart with rapture thrills,
   Like that above.

3. Let music swell the breeze,
   And ring from all the trees
   Sweet freedom's song;
   Let mortal tongues awake;
   Let all that breathe partake;
   Let rocks their silence break,
   The sound prolong.

4. Our fathers' God, to thee,
   Author of liberty,
   To thee we sing.
   Long may our land be bright
   With freedom's holy light;
   Protect us by thy might,
   Great God, our King!

6
America, the Beautiful

Katharine Lee Bates   *Samuel Augustus Ward*

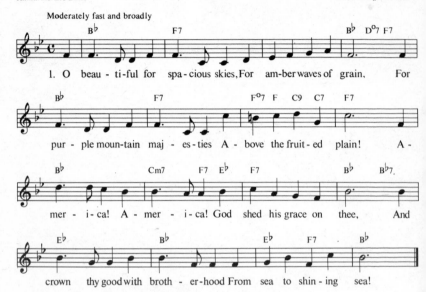

2. O beautiful for pilgrim feet,
   Whose stern, impassioned stress
   A thoroughfare for freedom beat
   Across the wilderness!
   America! America!
   God mend thine every flaw,
   Confirm thy soul in self-control,
   Thy liberty in law.

3. O beautiful for heroes proved
   In liberating strife,
   Who more than self their country loved,
   And mercy more than life!
   America! America!
   May God thy gold refine,
   Till all success be nobleness,
   And every gain divine.

4. O beautiful for patriot dream
   That sees beyond the years
   Thine alabaster cities gleam
   Undimmed by human tears!
   America! America!
   God shed his grace on thee,
   And crown thy good with brotherhood
   From sea to shining sea.

7

Angels, from the Realms of Glory

James Montgomery   *Henry Smart*

Moderately

1. An-gels, from the realms of glo - ry, Wing your flight o'er all the earth;

Ye who sang cre - a - tion's sto - ry Now pro-claim Mes - si - ah's birth:

Refrain

Come and wor-ship, Come and wor-ship, Wor-ship Christ the new-born King!

2. Shepherds, in the field abiding,
   Watching o'er your flocks by night,
   God with man is now residing;
   Yonder shines the infant light: (*Refrain*)

3. Sages, leave your contemplations;
   Brighter visions beam afar;
   Seek the great Desire of nations;
   Ye have seen his natal star: (*Refrain*)

4. Saints, before the altar bending,
   Watching long in hope and fear,
   Suddenly the Lord, descending,
   In his temple shall appear: (*Refrain*)

13

8
Au Clair de la Lune

French Folk Song

Brightly

1. Au clair de la lu - ne, Mon a - mi Pier - rot, Pré - te-moi ta plu - me Pour e-crire un mot Ma chan-dell' est mor - te, Je n'ai plus de feu, Ou-vre-moi ta por - te Pour l'a-mour de Dieu!

2. Au clair de la lune
   Pierrot répondit:
   "Je n'ai pas de plume;
   Je suis dans mon lit.
   Va chez la voisine,
   Je crois qu'elle y est,
   Car dans sa cuisine
   On bat le briquet."

3. Au clair de la lune
   Pierrot se rendort.
   Il rêve à la lune,
   Son coeur bat bien fort,
   Car toujours si bonne
   Pur l'enfant tout blanc,
   La lune lui donne
   Son croissant d'argent.

9

Auld Lang Syne

Traditional, Scottish

Moderately

1. Should auld ac-quaint-ance be for-got And nev - er brought to mind? Should

auld   ac-quaint-ance be   for-got, And days   of auld lang   syne?   For

auld___ lang___ syne, my friend, For   auld___ lang___ syne;   We'll

take   a cup of   kind - ness yet, For   auld___ lang ___ syne.

2. And here's a hand, my trusty friend,
   And give a hand of thine.
   We'll take a cup of kindness yet
   For auld lang syne.
   For auld lang syne, my friend,
   For auld lang syne.
   We'll take a cup of kindness yet
   For auld lang syne.

10
The Battle Hymn of the Republic

Julia Ward Howe   *Attr. to William Steffe*

2. I have seen him in the watchfires of a hundred circling camps;
   They have builded him an altar in the evening dews and damps;
   I can read his righteous sentence by the dim and flaring lamps;
   His day is marching on.

3. I have read a fiery gospel writ in burnished rows of steel:
   "As ye deal with my contemners, so with you my grace shall deal";
   Let the Hero, born of woman, crush the serpent with his heel,
   Since God is marching on.

4. He has sounded forth the trumpet that shall never call retreat;
   He is sifting out the hearts of men before his judgment seat.
   Oh, be swift, my soul, to answer him! Be jubilant, my feet!
   Our God is marching on.

5. In the beauty of the lilies Christ was born across the sea,
   With a glory in his bosom that transfigures you and me;
   As he died to make men holy let us die to make men free,
   While God is marching on.

11
A Bicycle Built for Two

Henry Dacre

Brightly

Dai - sy, Dai - sy, give me your an - swer, do. ___ I'm half cra - zy all for the love of you. ___ It won't be a styl - ish mar - riage, ___ I can't af - ford a car - riage; ___ But you'll look sweet up - on the seat of a bi - cy - cle built for two. ___

12
Bill Bailey

Hughie Cannon

Moderately fast

"Won't you come home, Bill Bail-ey,__ Won't you come home?"

She cries the whole night long._____

"I'll do the cook-ing, hon-ey,__ I'll pay the rent.

I know I've done you wrong._____ Re-mem-ber that

rain-y eve-ning I drove you out, with noth-ing but a fine-tooth

comb?_____ I know I'm to blame; Now, ain't that a

shame? Bill Bail-ey, won't you please come home?"_____

13
Blow the Man Down

Briskly

Call

American Sea Chantey

Response

I'll sing you a song, a good song of the sea, To me way,

18

aye, blow the man down; And trust that you'll join in the

Call

A7   Dm   G7   G7

cho-rus with me, Give me some time to blow the man down.

Response   F   C   G7 (+6)   C

2. 'Twas on board a Black Baller I first served my time,
   And away, hey, blow the man down;
   And on the Black Baller I wasted my prime.
   Give me some time to blow the man down.

3. It's when a Black Baller's preparing for sea,
   And away, aye, blow the man down;
   You'd split your sides laughing at the sights you would see,
   Give me some time to blow the man down.

4. With the tinkers and tailors and soldiers and all,
   To me way, aye, blow the man down;
   That ship as good seamen on board the Black Ball;
   Give me some time to blow the man down.

5. It's when a Black Baller is clear of the land,
   And away, hey, blow the man down;
   Our boatswain (bosun) then gives us the word of command.
   Give me some time to blow the man down.

6. It's larboard and starboard on the deck you will sprawl,
   And away, aye, blow the man down;
   For "Kicking" Jack Williams commands the Black Ball.
   Give me some time to blow the man down.

7. "Lay aft!" is the cry "to the break of the poop!"
   And away, hey, blow the man down;
   "Or I'll help you along with the toe of my boot."
   Give me some time to blow the man down.

8. Pay attention to orders, yes, you, one and all,
   To me way, aye, blow the man down;
   For see right above you there flies the Black Ball.
   Give me some time to blow the man down.

9. It's when a Black Baller comes down to the dock,
   And away, hey, blow the man down;
   The lasses and lads to the pier-heads do flock.
   Give me some time to blow the man down.

19

14
Buffalo Gals

Anonymous   *Adapted from a tune by Cool White*

Brightly

Verse

As I was walk-ing down the street, Down the street, down the street, A

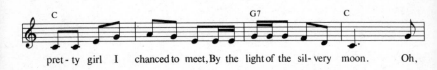

pret-ty girl I chanced to meet, By the light of the sil-very moon. Oh,

Chorus

Buf-fa-lo gals, won't you come out to-night, Come out to-night, come out to-night? Oh,

Buf-fa-lo gals, won't you come out to-night, And dance by the light of the moon?

2. I asked her if she'd stop and talk,
   Stop and talk, stop and talk;
   Her feet took up the whole sidewalk;
   She was fair to view. (*Chorus*)

3. I asked her if she'd be my wife,
   Be my wife, be my wife;
   Then I'd be happy all my life,
   If she'd marry me. (*Chorus*)

15
Clementine

Percy Montrose   *Attr. to Percy Montrose*

Brightly

In a cav-ern, in a can-yon, Ex-ca-va-ting for a mine, Lived a

min-er, for-ty-nin-er, And his daugh-ter, Clem-en-tine.

Chorus:

Oh my darling, oh my darling,
Oh my darling Clementine,
You are lost and gone forever,
Dreadful sorry, Clementine.

2. Light she was, and like a fairy,
And her shoes were number nine,
Herring boxes without topses,
Sandals were for Clementine.

3. Drove she ducklings to the water
Every morning just at nine,
Hit her foot against a splinter,
Fell into the foaming brine.

4. Ruby lips above the water,
Blowing bubbles soft and fine,
But, alas! I was no swimmer,
So I lost my Clementine.

5. In a churchyard near the canyon,
Where the myrtle doth entwine,
There grow roses and other posies,
Fertilized by Clementine.

6. In my dreams she still doth haunt me,
Robed in garments soaked with brine;
Though in life I used to hug her,
Now she's dead I draw the line.

7. Listen Boy Scouts, heed the warning
To this tragic tale of mine:
Artificial respiration
Could have saved my Clementine.

8. How I missed her, how I missed her,
How I missed my Clementine,
Till I kissed her little sister,
And forgot my Clementine.

16
Come and Go with Me

American Negro Gospel Song

Come and go with me to that land, Come and go with me to that land, Come and go with me to that land where I am bound. _____ Come and go with me to that land, Come and go with me to that land, Come and go with me to that land where I am bound. _____

2. There ain't no bowing in that land,
   Ain't no bowing in that land,
   Ain't no bowing in that land where I am bound.
   There ain't no bowing in that land,
   Ain't no bowing in that land,
   Ain't no bowing in that land where I am bound.

Continue, as above:

3. There ain't no kneeling in that land.

4. There ain't no poverty in that land.

5. There's love and brotherhood in that land.

6. There's peace and freedom in that land.

17
Come, Follow

Traditional English Round

Come, fol-low, fol-low, fol-low, fol-low, fol-low, fol-low me.

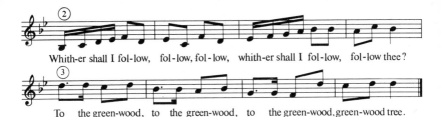

Whith-er shall I fol-low, fol-low, fol-low, whith-er shall I fol-low, fol-low thee?

To the green-wood, to the green-wood, to the green-wood, green-wood tree.

18
The Crawdad Song

Anonymous   *American Negro Folk Song*

Moderately fast

You get a line and I'll get a pole, hon-ey.

You get a line and I'll get a pole, babe.   You get a line and I'll get a pole;

We'll go down to the craw-dad hole,— hon-ey,— ba - by mine.

2. Yonder is a man with a pack on his back, honey,
   Yonder is a man with a pack on his back, babe,
   Yonder is a man with a pack on his back,
   Totin' all the crawdads he can pack,
   Honey, baby mine.

   Continue, as above:

3. A-settin' on the ice till my feet got hot,
   A-watchin' that crawdad rack and trot.

4. Whatcha gonna do when the lake runs dry?
   Sit on the bank and watch the crawdads die.

5. Whatcha gonna do when your man goes away?
   Get me a better one very next day.

19
Dear Lord and Father of Mankind

John Greenleaf Whittier

Frederick Charles Maker

Dear Lord and Fa-ther of man-kind, For-give our fool-ish ways; Re-clothe us in our right-ful mind, In pur-er lives thy ser-vice find, In deep-er rev-erence, praise.

2. In simple trust like theirs who heard,
   Beside the Syrian sea,
   The gracious calling of the Lord,
   Let us, like them, without a word,
   Rise up and follow thee.

3. O Sabbath rest by Galilee,
   O calm of hills above,
   Where Jesus knelt to share with thee
   The silence of eternity
   Interpreted by love.

4. With that deep hush subduing all
   Our words and works that drown
   The tender whisper of thy call,
   As noiseless let thy blessing fall
   As fell thy manna down.

5. Drop thy still dews of quietness,
   Till all our strivings cease;
   Take from our souls the strain and stress,
   And let our ordered lives confess,
   The beauty of thy peace.

20
Deck the Halls with Boughs of Holly

Traditional Welsh Carol

Brightly

Deck the halls with boughs of hol - ly, Fa la la la la, la la la la;

'Tis the sea - son to be jol - ly, Fa la la la la, la la la la.

Don we now our gay ap-par - el, Fa la la la la la la;

Troll the an - cient Yule-tide car - ol, Fa la la la la, la la la la.

2. See the blazing yule before us,
   Fa la la la la, la la la la,
   Strike the harp and join the chorus,
   Fa la la la la, la la la la,
   Follow me in merry measure,
   Fa la la, la la la, la la la,
   While I tell of Yuletide treasure,
   Fa la la la la, la la la la.

3. Fast away the old year passes,
   Fa la la la la, la la la la,
   Hail the new, ye lads and lasses,
   Fa la la la la, la la la la,
   Sing we joyous all together,
   Fa la la, la la la, la la la,
   Heedless of the wind and weather,
   Fa la la la la, la la la la.

21
Do, Lord, Remember Me

Optional verses by J.F.L.

American Negro Gospel Song

Moderately fast

Do, Lord, oh do, Lord, oh do re-mem-ber me.
Do, Lord, oh do, Lord, oh do re-mem-ber me.
Do, Lord, oh do, Lord, oh do re-mem-ber me.
Do, Lord, re - mem - ber me.

2. When I'm crossing Jordan,
Do remember me.
When I'm crossing Jordan,
Do remember me.
When I'm crossing Jordan,
Do remember me.
Do, Lord, remember me.

Continue, as above:

3. When I've got no friends at all.

4. When I'm bound in trouble.

5. When I'm goin' from door to door.

Optional verses:

When I wander from the path.

When I get to heaven, Lord.

When I'm scared and lonely, Lord.

When the day of judgment comes.

Paul and Silas bound in jail.

One did sing while the other did pray.

22
Down by the Riverside

American Negro Spiritual

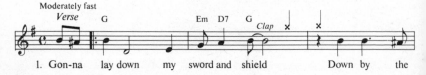

Moderately fast
Verse
Clap

1. Gon-na lay down my sword and shield Down by the

riv - er - side, Down by the riv- er- side, Down by the
riv- er - side. Gon- na lay down my sword and shield, Down by the

(Melody in lower notes)

riv - er - side, Down by the riv - er - side._____

Chorus

I ain't gon-na stud-y___ war no more, Ain't gon-na stud-y___ war no

more, Ain't gon-na stud- y___ war no more._____ I ain't gon-na

stud-y___ war no more, Ain't gon-na stud-y___ war no more. Ain't gon-na

(Melody in lower notes)

1.

Last verse

stud-y_____ war no more._____ 2. Gon-na more._____

2. Gonna join hands with everyone,
   Down by the riverside,
   Down by the riverside,
   Down by the riverside,
   Gonna join hands with everyone,
   Down by the riverside,
   Down by the riverside.

Continue, as above:

3. Gonna put on my long white robe.
4. Gonna put on my starry crown.
5. Gonna put on my golden shoes.
6. Gonna ride on a milk-white horse.
7. Gonna talk with the Prince of Peace.

27

23
Down in the Valley

American Folk Song

Moderately slow

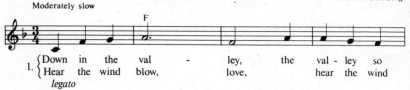

1. Down in the val - ley, the val - ley so
   Hear the wind blow, love, hear the wind

legato

low, _____ Late in the eve -
blow. _____

(Melody in lower notes)

ning, hear the wind blow. _____

2. If you don't love me, then love who you please,
   Throw your arms 'round me, give my heart ease.
   Give my heart ease, dear, give my heart ease,
   Throw your arms 'round me, give my heart ease.

3. Roses love sunshine, violets love dew;
   Angels in heaven know I love you.
   Know I love you, dear, know I love you,
   Angels in heaven know I love you.

4. Build me a castle forty feet high,
   So I can see him as he goes by.
   As he goes by, dear, as he goes by,
   So I can see him as he goes by.

5. Writing this letter, containing three lines,
   Answer my question, "Will you be mine?"
   "Will you be mine, dear, will you be mine?"
   Answer my question, "Will you be mine?"

Repeat first verse.

24
The Doxology

Thomas Ken (I)
William Kethe (II)

Attr. to Louis Bourgeois

Praise God, from whom all bless-ings flow; Praise him, all crea-tures here be-low; Praise

him a-bove, ye heaven-ly host; Praise Fa-ther, Son, and Ho-ly Ghost. A-men.

All peo-ple that on earth do dwell, Sing

to the Lord with cheer-ful voice. Him serve with mirth, his praise forth

tell, Come, ye be-fore him and re - joice.

25
Every Time I Feel the Spirit

American Negro Spiritual

Brightly
Chorus

Ev - ery time I____ feel the spir - it ____ Mov - ing in my heart,___

____ I will pray. Yes, ev - er - y time I____ feel the

Fine

spir - it____ Mov - ing in my heart,___ I will pray.____

Bass *(slowly, ad lib.)*

1. Up - on the moun - tain,____ when my Lord spoke,_____

a tempo
D.C.

____ Out of his mouth came____ fire and smoke._____

2. I looked around me;
   It looked so fine;
   I asked the Lord
   If it was mine.

   Chorus

3. There ain't but one train
   On this here track.
   It runs to Heaven,
   And it don't run back.

   Chorus

26
Everybody Loves Saturday Night

West African Folk Song

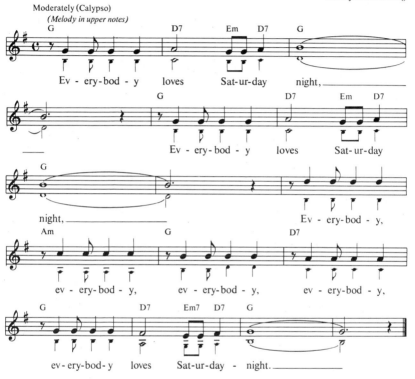

Selected verses, spelled phonetically:

French:

Too luh moanduh em Sahmehdee swahr.
Too luh moanduh em Sahmehdee swahr.
Too luh moanduh, too luh moanduh,
Too luh moanduh, too luh moanduh,
Too luh moanduh em Sahmehdee swahr.

Continue, as above:

German:

Yaydermahn leept Sahmstak Nahkt.

Greek:

Ohlee ahgahpoon toe Sahvahtoh Vrathee.

Italian:

Ohnyounoh amah Sahbahtoh nohtteh.

Norwegian:

Hehler vehrden elsker lurdahgskvel.

Russian:

Fsyeh lyubyat soobawtnyee vyeacher.

27
Ezekiel Saw the Wheel

American Negro Spiritual

E - ze-kiel saw the wheel, 'way up in the mid-dle of the air. E -

ze-kiel saw the wheel, 'way in the mid-dle of the air; And the

lit-tle wheel run by faith, and the big wheel run by the grace of God, A

wheel in a wheel (wheel in a wheel) 'way in the mid-dle of the air.

Verse

Some go to church for to sing and shout, 'way in the mid-dle of the air. Be -

fore six months they's shout-ed out. 'way in the mid-dle of the air.

32

2. Let me tell you what a hypocrite'll do,
   'Way in the middle of the air,
   He'll talk about me and he'll talk about you,
   'Way in the middle of the air.

Chorus

Continue, as above:

3. Don't pray for things that you don't need,
   The Lord don't like no sin and greed.

4. There's one thing sure that you can't do,
   You can't serve God and Satan, too.

5. One of these days about twelve o'clock,
   This old world's gonna reel and rock.

28
Fairest Lord Jesus

Anonymous   *Silesian Folk Tune*

Fair - est Lord Je - sus, Rul - er of all na - ture, O thou of
God and man the Son; Thee will I cher - ish,
Thee will I hon - or, Thou, my soul's glo - ry, joy, and crown.

2. Fair are the meadows,
   Fairer still the woodlands,
   Robed in the blooming
   Garb of spring;
   Jesus is fairer,
   Jesus is purer,
   Who makes the woeful
   heart to sing.

3. Fair is the sunshine,
   Fairer still the moonlight,
   And all the twinkling
   starry host.
   Jesus shines brighter,
   Jesus shines purer,
   Than all the angels
   heaven can boast.

29
The First Nowell

Traditional English Carol

Moderately

The_ first ___ Now - ell, the_ an - gel did say, Was to cer - tain poor shep-herds in fields as they lay; In _ fields _ where they lay_ keep-ing their sheep On a cold win - ter's night _ that

Refrain

was _ so deep. Now - ell, _ Now - ell, Now - ell, Now - ell, Born is the King_ of Is - ra - el.

2. They looked up and saw a star
   Shining in the East, beyond them far;
   And to the earth it gave great light,
   And so it continued both day and night.

   Refrain

3. This star drew nigh to the Northwest,
   O'er Bethlehem it took its rest,
   And there it did both stop and stay
   Right o'er the place where Jesus lay.

   Refrain

4. Then entered in those wisemen three,
   Full rev'rently on bended knee,
   And offered there in his presence,
   Their gold and myrrh and frankincense.

   Refrain

30
For the Beauty of the Earth

Folliot Sandford Pierpoint   *Conrad Kocher*

2. For the wonder of each hour
   Of the day and of the night,
   Hill and vale, and tree and flow'r,
   Sun and moon, and stars of light;
   Lord of all, to thee we raise
   This our hymn of grateful praise.

3. For the joy of human love,
   Brother, sister, parent, child,
   Friends on earth, and friends above,
   For all gentle thoughts and mild;
   Lord of all, to thee we raise
   This our hymn of grateful praise.

31
The Four Marys

British Ballad

Last night there were— four Ma - rys, To - night there'll be but three.___ There was Ma - ry Bea - ton and Ma - ry Sea - ton, And Ma - ry Car - mi -chael and me.___

2. Oh, often have I dressed my queen
   And put on her braw silk gown;
   But all the thanks I've got tonight
   Is to be hanged in Edinburgh town.

3. Full often have I dressed my queen;
   Put gold upon her hair;
   But I have got for my reward
   The gallows to be my share.

4. They'll tie a kerchief around my eyes
   That I may not see to dee;
   And they'll never tell my father or mother,
   But that I'm across the sea.

5. Last night there were four Maries,
   Tonight there'll be but three;
   There was Mary Beaton and Mary Seaton,
   And Mary Carmichael and me.

32
The Fox

British Ballad

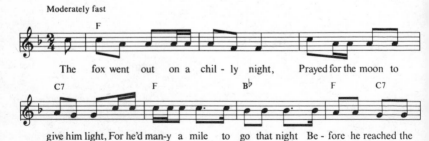

The fox went out on a chil - ly night, Prayed for the moon to give him light, For he'd man-y a mile to go that night Be - fore he reached the

town - o, the town - o, the town - o, He'd man-y a mile to

go that night Be - fore he reached the town - o.

2. He ran till he came to a great big pen
   Where the ducks and the geese were put therein,
   "A couple of you will grease my chin
   Before I leave this town-o,

   This town-o, this town-o,
   A couple of you will grease my chin
   Before I leave this town-o.

   Continue, as above:

3. He grabbed the gray goose by the neck,
   Throwed a duck across his back;
   He didn't mind their quack, quack, quack,
   And their legs all dangling down-o (*etc.*)

4. The old mother Flipper-Flopper jumped out of bed,
   Out of the window she cocked her head,
   Crying, "John, John, the gray goose is gone,
   And the fox is on the town-o" (*etc.*)

5. Then John, he went to the top of the hill,
   Blowed his horn both loud and shrill;
   The fox, he said, "I better flee with my kill
   Or they'll soon be on my trail-o" (*etc.*)

6. He ran till he came to his cozy den;
   There were the little ones, eight, nine, ten.
   They said, "Daddy, better go back again,
   For it must be a mighty fine town-o" (*etc.*)

7. Then the fox and his wife without any strife
   Cut up the goose with a fork and knife;
   They never had such a supper in their life,
   And the little ones chewed on the bones-o (*etc.*)

33
Frère Jacques

Traditional French Round, Adapted

Moderately fast

Frè - re Jac-ques, frè - re Jac-ques, Dor-mez–vous? dor-mez–vous?

Son-nez les ma-ti - nes, son-nez les ma-ti - nes, Din, din, don; din, din, don.

English version:
Are you sleeping, are you sleeping,
Brother John, brother John?
Morning bells are ringing, morning bells are ringing,
Ding dong, ding, ding, dong, ding.

Spanish version:
Fray Felipe, Fray Felipe,
Duermus tu, duermus tu?
Toca la campana, toca la campana,
Tan, tan, tan; tan, tan, tan.

German version:
Onkel Jakob, Onkel Jakob,
Schlafst du noch, schlafst du noch,
Ringe an der Glocke, ringe an der Glocke,
Bim bam, bom; bim, bam, bom.

34
Froggie Went A-Courting

British Ballad

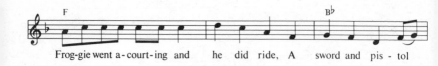

Brightly

F / Bb F (Ah hah) / Bb F (Ah hah)

Frog-gie went a-court-ing and he did ride, A - hum, a - hum.

F / Bb

Frog-gie went a-court-ing and he did ride, A sword and pis - tol

by   his   side,   A - hum,   a - hum.

2. He rode up to Miss Mousie's door,
   A-hum, a-hum,
   He rode up to Miss Mousie's door,
   Where he had often been before.
   A-hum, a-hum.

3. He said: "Miss Mouse, are you within?"
   A-hum, a-hum,
   He said: "Miss Mouse, are you within?"
   "Just lift the latch and do come in"
   A-hum, a-hum.

Continue, as above:

4. He took Miss Mousie on his knee,
   And said: "Miss Mouse, will you marry me?"

5. "Without my Uncle Rat's consent,
   I would not marry the President."

6. Now, Uncle Rat, when he came home,
   Said: "Who's been here since I've been gone?"

7. "A very fine gentleman has been here,
   He wishes me to be his dear."

8. Then Uncle Rat laughed and shook his sides,
   To think his niece would be a bride.

9. Then Uncle Rat, he went to town
   To buy his niece a wedding gown.

10. Where will the wedding breakfast be?
    Way down yonder in a hollow tree.

11. What will the wedding breakfast be?
    Two green beans and a black-eyed pea.

12. The first to come was the bumble bee.
    He danced a jig with Miss Mousie.

13. The next to come was Mister Drake,
    He ate up all of the wedding cake.

14. They all went sailing on the lake,
    And they all were swallowed by a big black snake.

15. So, that's the end of one, two, three,
    The rat, the frog, and Miss Mousie.

16. There's bread and cheese upon the shelf.
    If you want anymore just sing it yourself.

35
Go Down, Moses

American Negro Spiritual

2. Thus saith the Lord, bold Moses said:
   Let my people go.
   If not I smite your firstborn dead.
   Let my people go.

   Chorus

   Continue, as above:

3. No more shall they in bondage toil,
   Let them come out with Egypt's spoil.

4. Oh, Moses, the cloud shall cleave the way,
   A fire by night, a shade by day.

5. Your foes shall not before you stand,
   And you'll possess fair Canaan's land.

36
Go Tell Aunt Rhody

American Folk Song

Go   tell Aunt Rho - dy The old gray goose is dead.

2. The one she's been savin',
   The one she's been savin',
   The one she's been savin'
   To make a feather bed.

Continue, as above:

3. She died in the millpond,
   Standin' on her head.

4. The goslins are cryin',
   Because their mommy's dead.

5. Go tell Aunt Rhody,
   The old gray goose is dead.

37

Go, Tell It on the Mountain

American Negro Spiritual

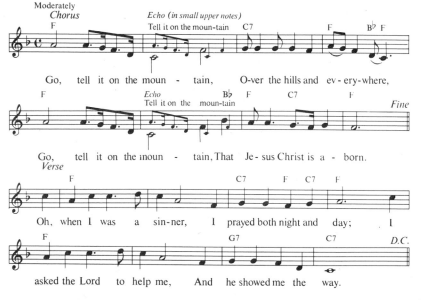

Go, tell it on the moun - tain, O-ver the hills and ev - ery-where,

Go, tell it on the moun - tain, That Je - sus Christ is a - born.

Oh, when I was a sin-ner, I prayed both night and day; I

asked the Lord to help me, And he showed me the way.

2. When I was a seeker,
   I sought both night and day;
   I asked my Lord to help me,
   And he taught me to pray.

   Chorus

3. He made me a watchman
   Upon the city wall;
   And if I am a Christian,
   I am the least of all.

   Chorus

4. It was in a lowly manger
   That **Jesus Christ** was born;
   The Lord sent down an angel
   That bright and glorious morn.

   Chorus

38

God Rest You Merry, Gentlemen

Traditional English Carol
Arr. by John Stainer

Moderately fast

1. God rest you mer - ry, gen - tle - men, Let noth - ing you dis -
2. From God our heav'n - ly Fa - ther A bless - ed an - gel

may, Re - mem - ber Christ our Sav - ior, Was born on Christ-mas
came; And un - to cer - tain shep - herds Brought tid - ings of the

Day; To save us all from Sa - tan's pow'r When we were gone a -
same; How that in Beth - le - hem was born The Son of God by

Refrain

stray. O—— tid - ings of com - fort and joy, com-fort and
name.

joy; O—— tid - ings of com - fort and joy.

3. "Fear not, then," said the angel,
Let nothing you affright,
This day is born a savior
Of a pure virgin bright,
To free all those who trust in him
From satan's power and might."

Refrain

4. Now to the Lord sing praises,
All you within this place,
And with true love and brotherhood
Each other now embrace;
This holy tide of Christmas
All others doth deface.

Refrain

39
Goin' Down the Road Feeling Bad

American Folk Song

Lively

I'm go-in' down the road feel-in' bad,_____ Lord, I'm

go-in' down the road feel-in' bad._____ I'm

go-in' down the road feel-in' bad, Lord.__ Lord, And I

ain't gon - na be treat- ed this - a - way._____

2. I'm goin' where the climate suits my clothes,
   I'm goin' where the climate suits my clothes,
   I'm goin' where the climate suits my clothes, Lord, Lord,
   And I ain't gonna be treated this a-way.

Continue, as above:

3. I'm a-lookin' for a job with honest pay.

4. These two-dollar shoes hurt my feet.

5. But ten-dollar shoes fit 'em neat.

6. I'm down in the jailhouse on my knees.

7. I'm leaving and I'm never coming back.

40
Good King Wenceslas

John M. Neale   *Traditional, European*

Moderately brisk

Good King Wen-ces - las looked out On the Feast of Ste - phen,

When the snow lay round a - bout, Deep and crisp, and e - ven:

Bright-ly shone the moon that night, Though the frost was cru - el,

When a poor man came in sight, Gath'-ring win - ter fu - el.

2. "Hither, Page, and stand by me,
   If thou knows't it; telling,
   Yonder peasant, who is he?
   Where and what his dwelling?"
   "Sire, he lives a good league hence,
   Underneath the mountain;
   Right against the forest fence,
   By Saint Agnes' fountain."

3. "Bring me flesh, and bring me wine,
   Bring me pine logs hither;
   Thou and I will see him dine,
   When we bear them thither."
   Page and monarch forth they went,
   Forth they went together;
   Through the rude wind's wild lament,
   And the bitter weather.

4. "Sire, the night is darker now,
   And the wind blows stronger;
   Fails my heart, I know not how,
   I can go no longer."
   "Mark my footsteps, my good page,
   Tread thou in them boldly:
   Thou shalt find the winter's rage,
   Freeze thy blood less coldly."

5. In his master's steps he trod,
   Where the snow lay dinted;
   Heat was in the very sod
   Which the Saint had printed.
   Therefore, Christian men, be sure,
   Wealth or rank possessing,
   Ye who now will bless the poor,
   Shall yourselves find blessing.

41
Good News

Moderately fast and rhythmic

American Negro Spiritual

2. There's a long white robe in heaven I know.

3. There's a starry crown in heaven I know.

4. There's a golden harp in heaven I know.

5. It's a better place than this world I know.

42

The Gospel Train

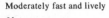

American Negro Spiritual

Moderately fast and lively

Verse

The gos-pel train is com-ing; I hear it just at hand; I

hear the wheels a - mov-ing and rum-bling thro' the land. Get on

board, lit-tle chil-dren; Get on board, lit-tle chil-dren; Get on

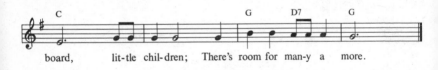

board, lit-tle chil-dren; There's room for man-y a more.

2. I hear the bell and whistle,
   A-comin' 'round the curve;
   She's playing all her steam and power
   And straining every nerve.

3. No signal for another train
   To follow on the line,
   Oh, sinner, you're forever lost
   If once you're left behind.

4. She's coming to the station,
   Oh, sinner, don't be vain,
   But come and get your ticket,
   And be ready for the train.

5. The fare is cheap and all can go,
   The rich and poor are there,
   No second-class on board the train,
   No difference in the fare.

6. We soon shall reach the station,
   Oh, how we then will sing,
   With all the heavenly army,
   We'll make the welkin ring.

43
The Great Meat Pie

British Folk Song

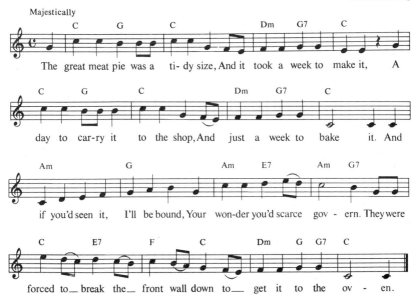

Majestically

The great meat pie was a ti-dy size, And it took a week to make it, A day to car-ry it to the shop, And just a week to bake it. And if you'd seen it, I'll be bound, Your won-der you'd scarce gov - ern. They were forced to_ break the_ front wall down to_ get it to the ov - en.

2. It took full thirty sacks of flour,
   It's a fact now that I utter,
   Three hundred pails of water, too,
   And a hundred tubs of butter.
   The crust was nearly seven feet thick,
   You couldn't easily bruise it,
   And the rolling pin was such a size
   It took ten men to use it.

3. There were twenty-five spareribs of pork,
   I'm sure I'm not mistaken,
   With two and thirty hams from York,
   And twenty sides of bacon.
   The pie was made by fifty cooks,
   And all of them first raters,
   And then they filled up all the nooks
   With a ton of kidney 'taters.

44

Green Grow the Lilacs

Irish-American Folk Song

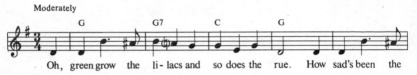

Oh, green grow the li-lacs and so does the rue. How sad's been the

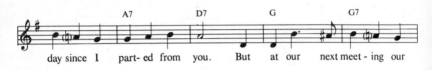

day since I part-ed from you. But at our next meet-ing our

(Melody in lower notes)

love we'll re-new, We'll change the green li-lacs for the red, white, and blue.

2. I once had a sweetheart but now I have none;
   He's gone off and left me to live here alone.
   He's gone off and left me contented to be;
   He must love another girl better than me.

3. I passed my love's window both early and late,
   The look that he gave me it made my heart ache.
   The look that he gave me was painful to see,
   For he loves another one better than me.

4. I wrote my love letters in red rosy lines,
   He sent me an answer all twisted in twines,
   Saying, "Keep your love letters and I will keep mine.
   Just you write to your love and I'll write to mine."

5. On top of the mountain where green lilacs grow,
   And over the valley where the still waters flow,
   I met my true love and he proved to be true.
   We changed the green lilacs for the Red, White, and Blue.

45
Green Grow the Rushes

English Folk Song

Moderately fast

1. I sing you one O, Green grow the rush-es O. What is your one O?

Green grow the rush-es O. One is one and all a-lone And ev-er-more shall be so.

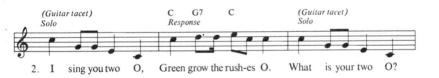

2. I sing you two O, Green grow the rush-es O. What is your two O?

Green grow the rush-es O. Two for the lil-y-white boys Cloth-ed all in green O.

One is one and all a-lone And ev-er-more shall be so. 3. I sing you three O.

Green grow the rush-es O. What is your three O? Green grow the rush-es O.

Three, three, the riv - als, Two for the lil-y-white boys Cloth-ed all in green O.

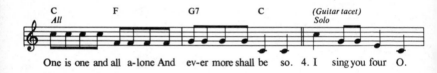

One is one and all a-lone And ev-er more shall be so. 4. I sing you four O.

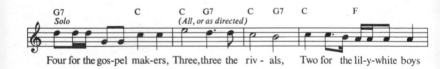

Green grow the rush-es O. What is your four O? Green grow the rush-es O.

Four for the gos-pel mak-ers, Three, three the riv - als, Two for the lil-y-white boys

Cloth-ed all in green O, One is one and all a-lone And ev-er-more shall be so.

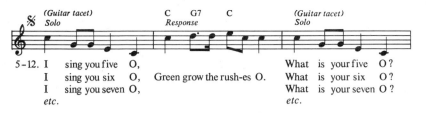

(Guitar tacet)
Solo — C G7 C Response — *(Guitar tacet)* Solo

5–12. I sing you five O, — What is your five O?
I sing you six O, Green grow the rush-es O. What is your six O?
I sing you seven O, What is your seven O?
etc. *etc.*

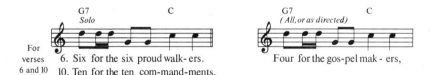

C G7 C
Response

Green grow the rush-es O.

Guitar (see note * and ** below)
Solo (ad lib.)

For verses 5, 7, 8, 9, 11, 12.

5. Five for the symbols at your door.
7. Seven for the seven stars in the sky.
8. Eight for the April rainers.
9. Nine for the nine bright shiners.
11. Eleven for the eleven who went to heaven.
12. Twelve for the twelve apostles.

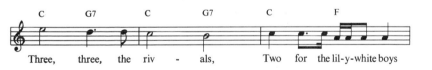

G7 C
Solo

G7 C
(All, or as directed)

For verses 6 and 10

6. Six for the six proud walk-ers.
10. Ten for the ten com-mand-ments.

Four for the gos-pel mak-ers,

C G7 C G7 C F

Three, three, the riv - als, Two for the lil-y-white boys

D7 G7 C F G7 C
All

Cloth-ed all in green O. One is one and all a-lone And ev-er-more shall be so.

*Use sustained C Chord throughout if preferred
**If guitar uses the chord changes, they are: C F B♭9 C

46
Greensleeves

Traditional English Folk Song

Moderately slow (in two)

A - las! my love,__you do me wrong__To cast me off__ dis-cour-teous-ly; And

I have lov - ed you so long__De - light - ing in__ your com - pa - ny.

Green - sleeves__was all my joy,____ Green - sleeves__was my de-light.

Green - sleeves was my heart of gold,__And who but my la-dy Green-sleeves.

2. I have been ready at your hand,
   To grant whatever you would crave;
   I have waged both life and land,
   Your love and good-will for to have.

3. If you intend thus to disdain,
   It does the more enrapture me,
   And even so, I still remain
   A lover in captivity.

4. My men were clothed all in green,
   And they did ever wait on thee;
   All this was gallant to be seen;
   And yet thou wouldst not love me.

5. Thou couldst desire no earthly thing
   But still thou hadst it readily.
   Thy music still to play and sing;
   And yet thou wouldst not love me.

6. Well, I will pray to God on high,
   That thou my constancy mayst see,
   And that yet once before I die,
   Thou wilt vouchsafe to love me.

7. Ah, Greensleeves, now farewell, adieu,
   To God I pray to prosper thee,
   For I am still thy lover true,
   Come once again and love me.

47

The Gypsy Rover

Irish Ballad

The gyp-sy rov-er came o-ver the hill, And down thro' the val-ley so

shad - y. He whis-tled and he sang till the green woods rang And he

won the heart of a la - dy. Ah dee doo, ah dee

do da day. Ah dee do, ah dee day dee. He whis-tled and he sang till the

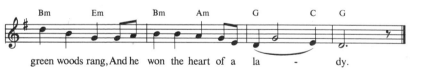

green woods rang, And he won the heart of a la - dy.

2. She left her father's castle gate;
   She left her own true lover;
   She left her servants and her estate
   To follow the gypsy rover.

3. Her father saddled his fastest steed
   And roamed the valley all over.
   He sought his daughter at great speed,
   And the whistling gypsy rover.

4. He came at last to a mansion fine
   Down by the River Clayde;
   And there was music and there was wine
   For the gypsy and his lady.

5. "He's no gypsy, my father," said she,
   "He's lord of freelands all over;
   And I will stay till my dying day
   With my whistling gypsy rover."

48
Hallelujah

Palestinian Folk Song

Very fast

Hal - le - lu - jah, hal - le - lu - jah, hal - le - lu - jah, hal - le - lu! Hal - le - lu - jah,

hal - le - lu - jah, hal - le - lu - jah, hal - le - lu! Hal - le - lu - jah, hal - le - lu!

Hal - le - lu - jah, hal - le - lu! Hal - le - lu - jah, hal - le - lu - jah, hal - le - lu - jah, hal - le - lu!

49

Hark! the Herald Angels Sing

Charles Wesley
Alt. by George Whitefield

Felix Mendelssohn
Adapted by William H. Cummings

Moderately slow and joyfully

Hark! the her - ald an - gels sing, __ "Glo - ry to the new - born King;

Peace on earth, and mer - cy mild, __ God and sin - ners rec - on - ciled!"

Joy - ful, all ye na - tions, rise, __ Join the tri - umph of the skies; __

With th'an - gel - ic host pro - claim, "Christ is __ born in Beth - le - hem!"

Refrain

Hark! the her - ald an - gels sing, "Glo - ry __ to the new - born King!"

54

2. Christ, by highest heav'n adored;
   Christ, the everlasting Lord!
   Late in time behold him come,
   Offspring of the virgin's womb.
   Veiled in flesh the Godhead see;
   Hail th'Incarnate Deity,
   Pleased as man with men to dwell,
   Jesus, our Emmanuel. (*Refrain*)

3. Hail! the heaven-born Prince of Peace!
   Hail the Sun of Righteousness!
   Light and life to all he brings,
   Risen with healing in his wings,
   Mild he lays his glory by,
   Born that man no more may die,
   Born to raise the sons of earth,
   Born to give them second birth. (*Refrain*)

50

Heaven Is So High

American Negro Gospel Song

Heav-en is so high, you can't get o-ver it, So low you
can't get un-der it, So wide you can't get a-round it; You
must come in at the door. You might as well just make
up your mind. You must come in at the door. Broth-er,
soon-er or lat-er you're bound to find, You must come in at the door.

2. There's only one path that takes you there,
   It leads right up to the door;
   It's narrow and straight, but it's free from care,
   You must come in at the door.

3. If you get there before I do,
   You must come in at the door,
   Don't worry or wait, I'm coming, too,
   You must come in at the door.

4. You'll find it's always open wide,
   You must come in at the door;
   So, brother, don't stop till you're inside;
   You must come in at the door.

51

Here We Come A-wassailing

Traditional British Carol

Moderately fast

2. We are not daily beggars
   That beg from door to door;
   But we are neighbors' children,
   Whom you have seen before. (*Refrain*)

3. God bless the master of this house,
   Likewise the mistress, too;
   And all the little children,
   That round the table go. (*Refrain*)

4. And all your kin and kinfolk
   That dwell both far and near,
   We wish a Merry Christmas
   And Happy New Year. (*Refrain*)

52

He's Got the Whole World in His Hands

Add.lyrics J.F.L.

American Negro Spiritual

Moderately and rhythmically

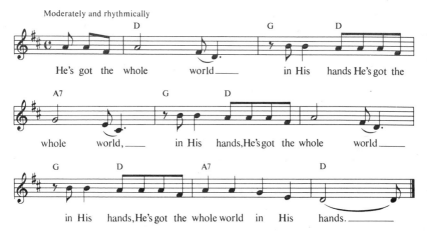

He's got the whole world____ in His hands He's got the whole world,____ in His hands, He's got the whole world____ in His hands, He's got the whole world in His hands.____

2. He's got the little bitty babies in his hands,
   He's got the little bitty babies in his hands,
   He's got the little bitty babies in his hands,
   He's got the whole world in his hands.

3. He's got you and me, brother, in his hands,
   He's got you and me, sister, in his hands,
   He's got you and me, brother, in his hands,
   He's got the whole world in his hands.

4. He's got the gamblin' man in his hands,
   He's got the gamblin' man in his hands,
   He's got the gamblin' man in his hands,
   He's got the whole world in his hands.

Additional verses, as above:

Drinkin' man

Worldly sinners

Cheaters and liars

Rich and poor

Meek and humble

53
Hey! Ho! Nobody Home

Traditional English Round

Briskly

① Hey! ho! No - bod - y home.

② Meat or drink or mon - ey have I none.

③ Yet will I be mer - ry, mer - ry, mer - ry, mer - ry.

54
Hey Lollee

Verses: J.F.L.

West Indian Folk Song
Adapted by J.F.L.

Moderately fast calypso
Chorus

Hey Lol-lee, lol - lee, lol-lee, Hey Lol-lee, lol - lee lo.—

Hey Lol-lee, lol - lee, lol-lee, Hey lol-lee, lol-lee lo.— *Fine*

Verse
Call

1. This is a cra-zy kind of song,— *Response* Hey lol-lee, lol - lee lo.— *Call* You

58

make it up as you go a - long, Hey Lol - lee, lol - lee lo.

2. When calypso singers sing this song,
   Hey lollee, lollee lo.
   It sometimes lasts the whole day long,
   Hey lollee, lollee lo.

3. First you invent a simple line,
   Hey lollee, lollee lo,
   Then another one to rhyme,
   Hey lollee, lollee lo.

55
The Hokey Pokey

American Folk Song

Moderately and rhythmically

You put your right foot in,— You put your right foot out,—You put your

right foot in — And shake it all a-bout. And then you do the hok-ey pok-ey and you

turn your-self a-bout; And that's what it's all a - bout. Hey!

2. You put your left foot in,
   You put your left foot out,
   You put your left foot in
   And shake it all about,
   And then you do the hokey pokey
   And you turn yourself about;
   And that's what it's all about.

Continue, as above:

3. Right hand.

4. Left hand.

5. Right shoulder.

6. Left shoulder.

7. Right hip.

8. Left hip.

9. Whole self.

56
Holy, Holy, Holy

Reginald Heber   *John Bacchus Dykes*

Ho-ly, ho-ly, ho - ly! Lord God al - might - y! Ear - ly in the

morn - ing our song shall rise to thee; Ho-ly, ho-ly, ho - ly,

mer - ci-ful and might - y; God in three per- sons, bless-ed Trin - i - ty.

2. Holy, holy, holy! All the saints adore thee,
   Casting down their golden crowns around the glassy sea;
   Cherubim and seraphim falling down before thee,
   Which wert, and art, and evermore shalt be.

3. Holy, holy, holy! Though the darkness hide thee,
   Though the eye of sinful man thy glory may not see;
   Only thou art holy; there is none beside thee,
   Perfect in power, in love, and purity.

4. Holy, holy, holy! Lord God Almighty!
   All thy works shall praise thy name in earth and sky and sea;
   Holy, holy, holy! merciful and mighty;
   God in three persons, blessed Trinity!

57
I Am a Pilgrim

American Gospel Song

I am a pil - grim,___ and a stran - ger,___

___ Trav-eling through _____ this wea-ri-some land._____

I got a home___ in _____ that yon-der cit - y, Oh

Lord, and it's not made, not made by hand._____

2. I got a mother, a sister, and a brother,
   Who have gone to that sweet land.
   I'm determined to go and see them, good Lord,
   All over on that distant shore.

3. As I go down to that river of Jordan,
   Just to bathe my weary soul,
   If I could touch but the hem of his garment, good Lord,
   Well, I believe it would make me whole.

58
I Couldn't Hear Nobody Pray

American Negro Spiritual

Moderately slow

I could-n't hear no-bod-y pray; Oh, I could-n't hear no-bod-y pray. Oh, way down yon-der by my-self, Oh, I could-n't hear no-bod-y pray(all a - lone),__ could-n't hear no-bod-y pray(kneel-ing down),__ could-n't hear no-bod-y pray, I could-n't hear no-bod-y pray, Oh, I could-n't hear no-bod-y pray, Oh, way down yon-der by my-self, Oh, I could-n't hear no-bod-y pray.

59
I Heard the Bells on Christmas Day

Henry Wadsworth Longfellow

J. Baptiste Calkin

Moderately

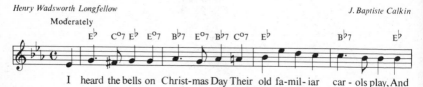

I heard the bells on Christ-mas Day Their old fa-mil-iar car-ols play, And

wild   and sweet the   words   re-peat   of   peace on earth, good   will   to men.

2. I thought how, as the day had come,
   The belfries of all Christendom
   Had rolled along th' unbroken song
   Of peace on earth, good will to men.

3. And in despair I bow'd my head:
   "There is no peace on earth," I said,
   "For hate is strong, and mocks the song
   Of peace on earth, good will to men."

4. Then pealed the bells more loud and deep:
   "God is not dead, nor doth he sleep;
   The wrong shall fail, the right prevail,
   With peace on earth, good will to men."

5. Till, ringing, singing on its way,
   The world revolved from night to day,
   A voice, a chime, a chant sublime,
   Of peace on earth, good will to men!

60
I Know Where I'm Going

British Folk Song

Moderately slow with feeling

I know where I'm   go-ing,___   And   I know who's go-in' with me;

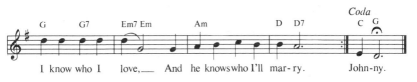

I know who I   love,___   And   he knows who I'll mar-ry.   John-ny.

2. I'll give up silk stockings,
   And shoes of bright green leather,
   Combs to buckle my hair,
   And rings for every finger.

3. Feather beds are soft,
   And painted rooms are bonnie;
   But I would trade them all
   For my handsome, winsome Johnny.

4. Some say he's a bad one,
   But I say he is bonnie.
   Fairest of them all
   Is my handsome, winsome Johnny.

Repeat first verse.

61
I Love the Mountains

American Folk Song

Boom de ah da, boom de ah da da, Boom, Boom, Boom; Boom, Boom!

62

I Saw Three Ships

English Folk Song

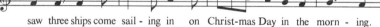

I saw three ships come sail-ing in on Christ-mas Day, on Christ-mas Day, I saw three ships come sail-ing in on Christ-mas Day in the morn-ing.

2. And what was in those ships all three,
   On Christmas Day, on Christmas Day?
   And what was in those ships all three,
   On Christmas Day in the morning?

3. The wise man three were in those ships,
   On Christmas Day, on Christmas Day.
   The wise men three were in those ships,
   On Christmas Day in the morning,

Continue, as above:

4. Pray, whither sailed those ships all three?

5. Oh, they sailed in to Bethlehem.

6. And all the angels in heaven shall sing.

7. And all the bells on earth shall ring.

8. And all the souls on earth shall sing.

9. Then let us all rejoice and sing.

63
I'm Gonna Sing When the Spirit Says Sing

American Negro Spiritual

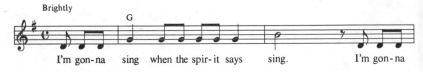

Brightly

I'm gon-na sing when the spir-it says sing. I'm gon-na

sing, when the spir-it says sing.___ I'm gon-na sing when the spir-it says

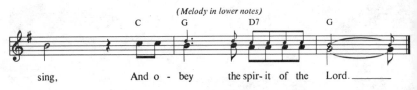

(Melody in lower notes)

sing, And o - bey the spir-it of the Lord.___

2. I'm gonna shout when the spirit says shout,
   I'm gonna shout when the spirit says shout,
   I'm gonna shout when the spirit says shout,
   And obey the spirit of the Lord.

Additional verses:

Preach.

Pray.

64
I'm on My Way

American Gospel Song

Moderately fast

I'm on my way___ and I won't turn back,___

_____ I'm on my way_____ and I won't turn back, _____

_____ I'm on my way_____ and I won't turn back, _____

_____ I'm on my way, great God, I'm on my way. _____

2. I asked my brother to come with me,
   I asked my brother to come with me,
   I asked my brother to come with me,
   I'm on my way, great God, I'm on my way.

Continue, as above:

3. If he won't come, I'll go alone.
4. I asked my sister to come with me.
5. If she won't come, I'll go alone.
6. I'll ask my boss to let me go.
7. If he says no I'll go anyhow.
8. I'm on my way to freedom land.

Optional verses:

I asked the judge to come with me.

But he was guilty, just like me.

I asked a rich man to come with me.

But he was too busy to take the time.

67

65
In the Pines

American Folk Song

Moderately slow

Verse

True love, true love, don't lie to me, Tell me where did you sleep last night?_____ I slept in the pines, where the sun nev-er shines And I shiv-ered when the cold wind

Chorus

blowed._____ To the pines, to the pines where the sun nev-er shines And you shiv-er when the cold wind_ blows. _____

2. You slighted me once; you slighted me twice;
   But you'll never slight me no more.
   You caused me to weep; you caused me to mourn;
   You caused me to leave my home. (*Chorus*)

3. Them long steel rails with short crossties
   Gonna carry me away from home.
   That lonesome track gonna take me back
   Where a man can call his soul his own. (*Chorus*)

4. The longest train I ever saw
   Was on the Georgia line.
   The engine passed at five o'clock;
   The caboose done passed at nine. (*Chorus*)

5. The longest day I every saw,
   Ever since I started to roam,
   Was the day I left my own true love,
   The day I left my home. (*Chorus*)

6. Now, don't you hear those mournin' dove
   Flyin' from pine to pine,
   Mournin' for their own true love
   Just like I mourn for mine. (*Chorus*)

66

It Came upon the Midnight Clear

Edmund H. Sears   *Richard Storrs Willis*

It came up-on__ the mid-night clear, That glo - rious song of old, __ From

an - gels bend - ing near the earth, To touch their harps of gold: __ "Peace

on the earth, good will to men, From heaven's all gra - cious King." __ The

world in sol - emn still - ness lay, To hear the an - gels sing. __

2. Still through the cloven skies they come
   With peaceful wings unfurled,
   And still their heavenly music floats
   O'er all the weary world:
   Above its sad and lowly plains
   They bend on hovering wing,
   And ever o'er its Babel sounds
   The blessed angels sing.

3. O ye, beneath life's crushing load,
   Whose forms are bending low,
   Who toil along the climbing way
   With painful steps and slow,
   Look now! for glad and golden hours
   Come swiftly on the wing:
   O rest beside the weary road,
   And hear the angels sing.

4. For lo! the days are hastening on,
   By prophets seen of old,
   When with the evercircling years,
   Shall come the time foretold,
   When peace shall over all the earth
   Its ancient splendors fling,
   And the whole world send back the song
   Which now the angels sing.

67

I've Been Workin' on the Railroad

American Folk Song
Adapted by J.F.L.

Moderately fast

I've been work-in' on the rail - road, All the live-long day;

I've been work-in' on the rail - road, Just to pass the time a - way.

Don't you hear the whis-tle blow - in'? Rise up so ear-ly in the morn.

Don't you hear the cap-tain shout - in', "Din - ah, blow your horn."

Di-nah, won't you blow, Di-nah, won't you blow, Di-nah, won't you blow your

horn?_____ Di-nah, won't you blow, Di-nah, won't you blow,

Di-nah, won't you blow your horn? Some-one's in the kitch-en with

Di - nah, Some-one's in the kitch-en, I know._____

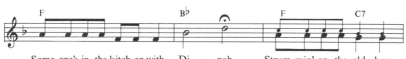

Some-one's in the kitch-en with Di - nah, Strum-min' on the old ban -

jo. Fee fi fid-dle-ee - i - o, Fee fi

fid-dle-ee-i - o,_____ Fee fi fid-dle-ee-i - o, Strum-min' on the old ban-

jo. Now you may think _____ that there ain't no more._____

_____ Oh, you may think _____ that there ain't no more._____

_____ Now you may think that there ain't no more, well, there ain't!

68
Jacob's Ladder

American White Spiritual
Adapted by J.F.L.

We are climb-ing Ja-cob's lad-der, We are

climb-ing Ja-cob's lad-der, We are climb-ing

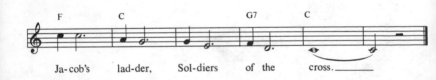

Ja-cob's lad-der, Sol-diers of the cross.____

2. Each rung takes us higher, higher,
   Each rung takes us higher, higher,
   Each rung takes us higher, higher,
   Soldiers of the cross.

Continue, as above

3. Sinner, do you love my Jesus?

4. If you love him, why not serve him?

5. We are climbing higher, higher.

69
Jingle Bells

Brightly

Chorus
(Melody in upper notes)

James S. Pierpont

Jin-gle bells, jin-gle bells, jin-gle all the way!

Oh, what fun it is to ride in a one-horse o-pen sleigh! Jin-gle bells, jin-gle bells,

jin-gle all the way! Oh, what fun it is to ride in a one-horse o-pen sleigh!

Dash-ing through the snow In a one-horse o-pen sleigh,

O'er the fields we go, Laugh-ing all the way. Bells on bob-tail ring,

Mak-ing spir-its bright. Oh, what fun it is to sing A sleigh-ing song to-night. Oh,

73

70

Johnny, I Hardly Knew You

Irish Folk Song

Slowly

With your guns and drums and drums and guns, hoo - roo, _____ hoo - roo, _____ With your guns and drums and drums and guns, hoo - roo, _____ hoo - roo, _____ With your guns and drums and drums and guns, The en - e - my near - ly slew you, Oh, my dar - ling dear, you look so queer, Oh John - ny, I hard - ly knew you.

2. Where are your eyes that were so mild, hooroo, hooroo,
   Where are your eyes that were so mild, hooroo, hooroo,
   Where are your eyes that were so mild
   When my heart you first beguiled;
   Oh, why did you run from me and the child?
   Johnny, I hardly knew you.

Continue, as above:

3. Where are your legs that used to run, *etc.*
   When first you went to carry a gun?
   Indeed your dancing days are done.
   Oh, Johnny, I hardly knew you.

4. You haven't an arm you haven't a leg, *etc.*
   You're a hopeless shell of a man with a peg.
   And you'll have to be put with a bowl to beg.
   Oh, Johnny, I hardly knew you.

5. It's glad I am to see you home, *etc.*
   My darlin', you're so pale and wan.
   So low in flesh, so high in bone . . .
   Oh, Johnny, I hardly knew you.

6. They're rollin' out the drums again, *etc.*
   But they'll never take my sons again,
   No, they'll never take my sons again,
   Johnny, I'm swearin' to you.

71

Joshua Fought the Battle of Jericho

American Negro Spiritual

Moderately fast and rhythmic

2. Well, the Lord done told old Joshua:
   "You must do just what I say,
   March 'round that city seven times
   And the walls will tumble away."

3. So up to the walls of Jericho,
   He marched with spear in hand,
   "Go blow them ram horns," Joshua cried,
   'Cause the battle is in my hand."

4. Then the lamb, ram, sheep horns began to blow,
   And the trumpet began to sound,
   Joshua told the children to shout, that mornin'
   And the walls came tumblin' down.

72
Joy to the World

Isaac Watts

*Arr. from George F. Handel
by Lowell Mason*

Joy to the world! the Lord is come; Let earth re-

ceive her King; Let ev-ery__ heart__ pre-pare__ him__

room, ___ And heaven and na-ture__ sing, And__ heaven and na-ture__

sing, And__ heaven, and heaven__ and na-ture sing.

2. Joy to the world! the Savior reigns.
   Let men their songs employ;
   While fields and floods, rocks, hills, and plains
   Repeat the sounding joy,
   Repeat the sounding joy,
   Repeat, repeat the sounding joy.

3. He rules the world with truth and grace,
   And makes the nations prove
   The glories of his righteousness,
   And wonders of his love,
   And wonders of his love,
   And wonders, wonders of his love.

73

Just a Closer Walk with Thee

American Gospel Song

Just a clos-er walk with thee,_____

Grant it, Je-sus, is my plea._____

Dai - ly walk-ing close with thee;_____ Let it

be, dear Lord, let it be._____

2. I am weak but thou art strong;
   Jesus, keep me from all wrong;
   I'll be satisfied as long,
   As I walk, dear Lord, close to thee.

3. Through this world of toil and snares,
   If I falter, Lord, who cares?
   Who with me my burden shares?
   None but thee, dear Lord, none but thee.

4. When my feeble life is o'er,
   Time for me will be no more;
   Guide me gently, safely on,
   To thy shore, dear Lord, to thy shore.

74
The Keeper Would A-Hunting Go

English Folk Song

Briskly

The keep-er would a - hunt-ing go, And un-der his coat he car-ried a bow,

All for to shoot at a mer-ry lit-tle doe, A-mong the leaves so__ green, O

Group One   Two   One   Two   All

Jack-ie boy! Mas-ter! Sing ye well? Ver-y well! Hey down! Ho down! Der-ry, der-ry down, A-

mong the leaves so__ green, O To me hey down, down, To me ho down, down.

Hey down, ho down, der-ry der-ry down A-mong the leaves so__ green O.

2. The first doe he shot at he missed;
   The second doe he trimmed he kissed;
   The third doe went where nobody wist
   Among the leaves so green, O.

3. The fourth doe she did cross the plain;
   The keeper fetched her back again;
   Where she is now she may remain
   Among the leaves so green, O.

4. The fifth doe she did cross the brook;
   The keeper fetched her back with his crook;
   Where she is now you must go and look
   Among the leaves so green, O.

5. The sixth doe she ran over the plain;
   But he with his hounds did turn her again,
   And it's there he did hunt in a merry, merry vein
   Among the leaves so green, O.

75
Kookaburra

Australian Round

Moderately slow

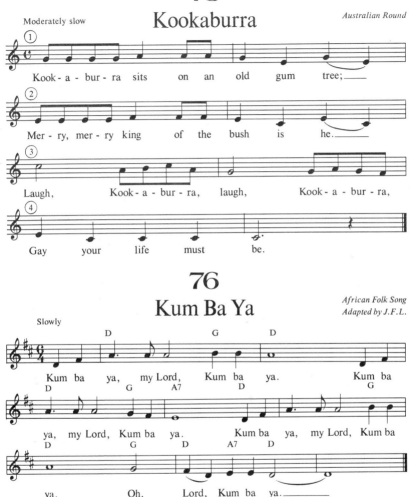

Kook - a - bur - ra sits on an old gum tree;____

Mer - ry, mer - ry king of the bush is he.____

Laugh, Kook - a - bur - ra, laugh, Kook - a - bur - ra,

Gay your life must be.

76
Kum Ba Ya

African Folk Song
Adapted by J.F.L.

Slowly

Kum ba ya, my Lord, Kum ba ya. Kum ba

ya, my Lord, Kum ba ya. Kum ba ya, my Lord, Kum ba

ya. Oh, Lord, Kum ba ya.____

Verses (same tune as chorus):

1. Someone's crying, Lord, kum ba ya,
   Someone's crying, Lord, kum ba ya,
   Someone's crying, Lord, kum ba ya,
   Oh, Lord, kum ba ya.

Chorus

Continue, as above:

2. Someone's singing, Lord, etc.

3. Someone's praying.

4. Someone's hoping.

77
Let Me Fly

American Negro Gospel Song

Verse

Way down yon-der in the mid-dle of the field, An-gel work-in' on the char-iot wheel. Not so par-ti-cu-lar 'bout work-in' at the wheel, But I just want-a see how the char-iot feels. Now let me fly,____ Now, let me fly.____ Now let me fly_ in-to Mount Zi-on, Lord, Lord.____

Chorus

2. I got a mother in the promised land,
   Ain't gonna stop till I shake her hand.
   Not so particular 'bout shakin' her hand,
   But I just wanta go up in the promised land.

3. Meet that hypocrite on the street,
   First thing he'll do is show his teeth.
   Next thing he'll do is to tell a lie,
   And the best thing to do is to pass him by.

78
Let My Little Light Shine

American Negro Gospel Song

Moderately fast

Chorus

This lit-tle light of mine, _ I'm gon-na let it shine;

79

Little Black Train Is A-comin'

American Negro Spiritual

Moderately fast
Introd.

Verse

God told Hez-e-ki-ah, In a mes-sage from on high: "Go

set your house in or-der For you will sure-ly die." He

turned to the wall a-weep-ing, oh, see the king in tears. He

got his bus-i-ness fixed all right, God spared him fif-teen years.

Chorus

Lit-tle black train is a-com-ing. Get all your bus-'ness right. Go

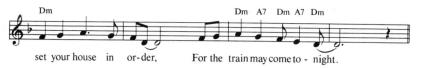

set your house in or-der, For the train may come to - night.

2. Go tell that ballroom lady,
   All filled with worldly pride,
   That a little black train is coming,
   Get prepared to take a ride.
   For the little black train and engine,
   Caboose and baggage car,
   And all the folks a-riding
   Got to stop at the judgment bar.

3. Did you see that man in darkness?
   Hid from the gospel light?
   Did you hear him scream for mercy
   When the train came moving in sight?
   The devil had him in shackles,
   Wrapped around his soul so tight,
   No time to fix his business
   When the train rolled in that night.

   Chorus

80
Lolly Too Dum

American Folk Song

Moderately fast

As I went out one morn-ing to take the morn-ing air, Lol-ly too dum, too dum, Lol-ly too dum day. As I went out one morn-ing to take the morn-ing air, I o-ver-heard a moth-er A-scold-ing her daugh-ter fair, Lol-ly too dum, too dum, Lol-ly too dum day.

2. "You better go wash them dishes,
And hush that clattering tongue,
Lolly too dum, too dum, lolly too dum day.
I know you want to get married
And that you are too young."
Lolly too dum, too dum, lolly too dum day.

Continue, as above:

3. "Oh, pity my condition
As you would your own,
For seventeen long years
I've been sleeping all alone."

4. "Yes, I'm seventeen and over,
And that you will allow—
I must and I will get married
For I'm in the notion now."

5. "Supposin' I was willin'.
Where would you get your man?"
"Why, Lordy mercy, Mammy,
I'd marry handsome Sam."

6. "Supposin' he should slight you
Like you done him before?"
"Why, Lordy mercy, Mammy,
I could marry forty more."

7. "There's peddlers and there's tinkers
And boys from the plow,
Oh Lordy mercy, Mammy,
I'm gettin' that feeling now!"

8. "Now my daughter's married
   And well fer to do,
   Gather 'round young fellers,
   I'm on the market too."

9. "Lordy mercy, Mammy,
   And who would marry you?
   Ain't no man alive wants
   A wife as old as you."

10. "There's doctors and there's lawyers
    And men of high degree,
    And some of them will marry
    And one will marry me."

11. "Now we both are married
    And well fer to be.
    Ha ha ha, you pretty young girls,
    That feeling's off of me."

81
Lonesome Road

American Negro Folk Song

Moderately slow

Look down, look down that lone - some road, Hang down your head and cry._____ The best of friends must part some - time, Then why not you and I?_____

2. Look down, look down that lonesome road,
   Before you travel on;
   Look up, look up and greet your Maker,
   'Fore Gabriel blows his horn.

3. Look down, look down, it's weary walkin',
   Trudgin' down that lonesome road.
   Look up, look up and greet your Maker,
   'Fore Gabriel blows his horn.

Repeat first verse.

82
Lonesome Valley

American Folk Hymn

Slowly

1. Je - sus walked ⸺ this lone-some val - ley, ⸺ He had to walk ⸺ it by him - self, Oh, no-bod-y else ⸺ could walk it for him. ⸺ He had to walk it by him - self.

2. You must go and stand your trial,
You have to stand it by yourself.
Oh, nobody else can stand it for you,
You have to stand it by yourself.

3. We must walk this lonesome valley,
We have to walk it by ourselves.
Oh, nobody else can walk it for us,
We have to walk it by ourselves.

83
Mary and Martha

American Negro Spiritual

Moderately fast
Verse

Mar-y and Mar-tha jus' gone 'long, Mar-y and Mar-tha jus' gone 'long,

(Melody in lower notes)

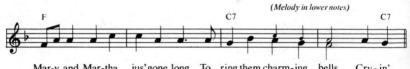

Mar-y and Mar-tha jus' gone long To ring them charm-ing bells. Cry-in',

Chorus

"Free grace, un-a-dy-in' love, Free grace, un-a-dy-in' love,

(Melody in lower notes)

Free grace, un-a-dy-in' love", To ring them charm-ing bells.

2. Father and mother jus' gone 'long,
   Father and mother jus' gone 'long,
   Father and mother jus' gone 'long,
   To ring them charming bells.

Continue, as above:

3. Preacher and the elder jus' gone 'long.

4. Everybody jus' gone 'long.

84
Michael, Row the Boat Ashore

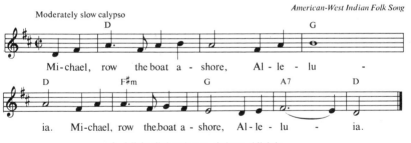

American-West Indian Folk Song

Moderately slow calypso

Mi-chael, row the boat a-shore, Al-le-lu - ia. Mi-chael, row the boat a-shore, Al-le-lu - ia.

2. Michael's boat's a music boat, Alleluia,
   Michael's boat's a music boat, Alleluia.

3. Sister, help to trim the sail, Alleluia,
   Sister, help to trim the sail, Alleluia.

4. Jordan's River is chilly and cold, Alleluia,
   Kills the body but not the soul, Alleluia.

5. Jordan's River is deep and wide, Alleluia,
   Meet my mother on the other side, Alleluia.

6. Gabriel, blow the trumpet horn, Alleluia,
   Blow the trumpet loud and long, Alleluia.

7. Brother, lend a helping hand, Alleluia,
   Brother, lend a helping hand, Alleluia.

8. Michael's boat's a gospel boat, Alleluia,
   Michael's boat's a gospel boat, Alleluia.

85
My Faith Looks up to Thee

Ray Palmer   *Lowell Mason*

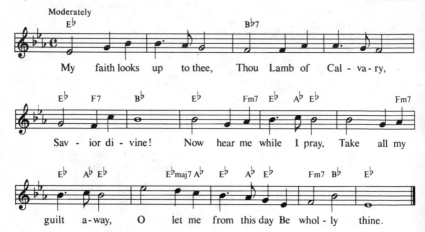

My faith looks up to thee, Thou Lamb of Cal-va-ry, Sav-ior di-vine! Now hear me while I pray, Take all my guilt a-way, O let me from this day Be whol-ly thine.

2. May thy rich grace impart
   Strength to my fainting heart,
   My zeal inspire;
   As thou hast died for me,
   O may my love to thee
   Pure, warm, and changeless be,
   A living fire!

3. While life's dark maze I tread,
   And griefs around me spread,
   Be thou my guide;
   Bid darkness turn to day,
   Wipe sorrow's tears away,
   Nor let me ever stray
   From thee aside.

4. When ends life's transient dream,
   When death's cold, sullen stream
   Shall o'er me roll;
   Blest Savior, then, in love,
   Fear and distrust remove;
   O bear me safe above,
   A ransomed soul!

86
My Gal Sal

Paul Dresser

Moderately

They called her friv-o-lous Sal, ____ A pe-cu-liar

sort of a gal, ____ With a heart that was mel-low, An

all-round good fel-low Was my old pal. ____

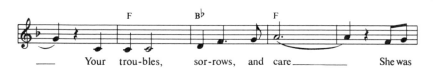

____ Your trou-bles, sor-rows, and care ____ She was

al-ways will-ing to share; ____ A wild sort of dev-il, But

dead on the lev-el, Was my gal Sal. ____

87

My Home's Across the Smoky Mountains

American Folk Song

My home's a - cross the Smok-y Moun - tains, My

home's a - cross the Smok-y Moun - tains, My

home's a - cross the Smok-y Moun - tains, And I'll

nev-er get to see you an - y - more, more, more, And I'll

nev-er get to see you an - y - more.

2. Goodbye, my honey, sugar darlin',
   Goodbye, my honey, sugar darlin',
   Goodbye, my honey, sugar darlin',
   And I'll never get to see you anymore, more, more,
   And I'll never get to see you anymore.

3. I love my honey, feed her candy,
   I love my honey, feed her candy,
   I love my honey, feed her candy,
   And I'll never get to see her anymore, more, more,
   Oh, I'll never get to see her anymore.

Repeat first verse.

88
New River Train

New lyrics by J.F.L.

American Folk Song

I'm rid-ing on that New Riv-er Train;_____ I'm rid-ing on that New Riv-er Train;_____ Same old train that__ brought me here Gon-na

(Melody in lower notes)

car-ry me home a - gain._____

2. Oh, baby, remember what you said;
   Oh, baby, remember what you said;
   Remember what you said: You would
     rather see me dead
   Than ridin' on that New River Train.

3. Oh, darlin', you can't love one,
   Oh, darlin', you can't love one;
   You can't love one and have any fun,
   Oh, darlin', you can't love one.

Continue, as above:

4. You can't love two and your little heart be true.

5. You can't love three and still love me.

6. You can't love four and love me anymore.

7. You can't love five and still stay alive.

8. You can't love six and not get in a fix.

9. You can't love seven if you want to go to heaven.

10. You can't love eight 'cause you'll make somebody wait.

11. You can't love nine and keep 'em all in line.

12. You can't love ten and stay out of the county pen.

13. You can't love eleven—you should've stopped at seven.

89
Nine Hundred Miles

American Folk Song

Moderately slow

Well, I'm walk-ing down this track, I've got tears in my eyes,
Tryin' to read a let-ter from my home, _____ And if this
train runs me right, I'll be home to-mor-row night, 'Cause I'm
nine hun-dred miles from my home, _____ And I
hate to hear that lone - some whis-tle blow. _____

Chorus

2. I will pawn you my watch;
   I will pawn you my chain;
   Pawn you my gold diamond ring.

   Chorus

3. If my woman tells me so,
   I will railroad no more;
   I'll hang around her shanty all the time.

   Chorus

4. Now this train I ride on
   Is a hundred coaches long;
   Travels back a hundred miles or more;

   Chorus

90

Nine Men Slept in a Boardinghouse Bed

American Folk Song

Briskly

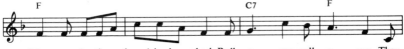

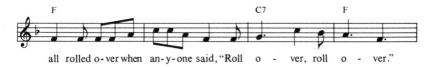

Nine men slept in a board-ing house bed, Roll o - ver, roll o - ver, They

all rolled o-ver when an-y-one said, "Roll o - ver, roll o - ver."

One of them tho't it would be a good joke,   Not to roll o-ver when an-y-one spoke,

And in the scuf-fle his neck was broke, Roll o - ver, roll o - ver.

2. Eight men slept in a boardinghouse bed,
   Roll over, roll over.
   They all rolled over when anyone said,
   "Roll over, roll over."
   One of them thought it would be a good joke,
   Not to roll over when anyone spoke,
   And in the scuffle his neck was broke,
   Roll over, roll over.

Continue, as above, until the bed is empty:
3. Seven men slept. . . .

91
Nobody Knows the Trouble I've Seen

Moderately slow
Chorus

American Negro Spiritual

No-bod-y knows the trou-ble I've seen, No-bod-y knows but Je - sus. No-bod-y knows the trou-ble I've seen, Glo - ry hal - le - lu - jah! Some-times I'm up, some-times I'm down, Oh, yes, Lord; Some-times I'm al-most to the ground, Oh, yes, Lord!

2. Now you may think that I don't know,
   Oh, yes, Lord,
   But I've had my troubles here below,
   Oh, yes, Lord!

   Chorus

   Continue, as above:

3. One day when I was walkin' along,
   The sky opened up and love came down.

4. What makes old Satan hate me so?
   He had me once and had to let me go.

5. I never shall forget that day,
   When Jesus washed my sins away.

92
Now the Day Is Over

Sabine Baring-Gould   *Joseph Barnby*

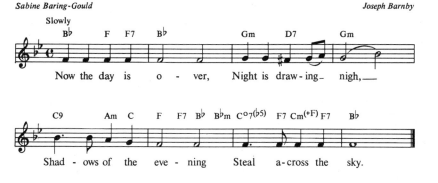

Now the day is o - ver, Night is draw-ing nigh,
Shad - ows of the eve - ning Steal a-cross the sky.

2. Through the hours of darkness,
   May thine angels spread
   Their white wings above me,
   Watching 'round my bed.

93
Now We'll Make the Rafters Ring

Words altered by J.F.L.

Traditional English Round

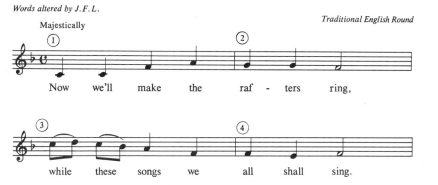

Now we'll make the raf - ters ring,
while these songs we all shall sing.

94
O Christmas Tree

German Folk Song

Briskly

O Christ-mas tree, O Christ-mas tree, With faith-ful leaves un-chang-ing. O Christ-mas tree, O Christ-mas tree, With faith-ful leaves un-chang-ing. Not on-ly green in sum-mer's heat, But al-so win-ter's snow and sleet; O Christ-mas tree, O Christ-mas tree, with faith-ful leaves un-chang-ing.

2. O Christmas tree, O Christmas tree,
   Of all the trees most lovely; (*Repeat*)
   Each year you bring to me delight
   Gleaming in the Christmas night.
   O Christmas tree, O Christmas tree,
   Of all the trees most lovely.

3. O Christmas tree, O Christmas tree,
   Your leaves will teach me also (*Repeat*)
   That hope and love and faithfulness
   Are precious things I can possess.
   O Christmas tree, O Christmas tree,
   Your leaves will teach me also.

Optional verse:

O Christmas tree, O Christmas tree,
How lovely are your branches. (*Repeat*)
In summer sun or winter snow
A coat of green you always show.
O Christmas tree, O Christmas tree.
How lovely are your branches.

95
O Come, All Ye Faithful

John Francis Wade (?)
Trans. and alt. by Frederick Oakeley

John Francis Wade

2. Sing, choirs of angels, sing in exultation,
   O Sing, all ye citizens of heaven above!
   Glory to God, all glory in the highest;

   Refrain

3. Yea, Lord, we greet thee, born this holy morning,
   Jesus, to thee be all glory giv'n!
   Word of the Father, now in flesh appearing;

   Refrain

96

O Little Town of Bethlehem

Phillips Brooks   *Lewis H. Redner*

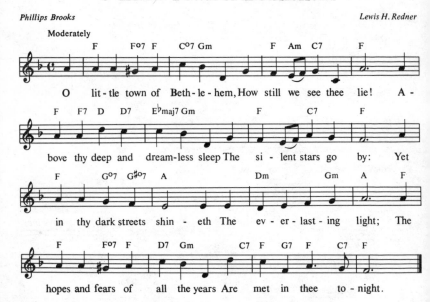

O lit-tle town of Beth-le-hem, How still we see thee lie! A-
bove thy deep and dream-less sleep The si-lent stars go by: Yet
in thy dark streets shin-eth The ev-er-last-ing light; The
hopes and fears of all the years Are met in thee to-night.

2. For Christ is born of Mary,
   And gathered all above,
   While mortals sleep, the angels keep
   Their watch of wondering love.
   O morning stars, together
   Proclaim the holy birth,
   And praises sing to God the King,
   And peace to men on earth!

3. How silently how silently
   The wondrous gift is given!
   So God imparts to human hearts
   The blessings of his heaven.
   No ear may hear his coming,
   But in this world of sin,
   Where meek souls will receive him, still
   The dear Christ enters in.

4. O holy Child of Bethlehem!
   Descend to us, we pray;
   Cast out our sin, and enter in,
   Be born in us today.
   We hear the Christmas angels
   The great glad tidings tell;
   O come to us, abide with us,
   Our Lord Emmanuel!

97

Oh, Dear, What Can the Matter Be?

English Folk Song

2. He promised to buy me a pair of sleeve buttons,
   A pair of new garters would cost him but tuppence,
   A pair of red stockings to go with the ribbons
   That tie up my bonny brown hair.

3. He promised he'd bring me a basket of posies,
   A garland of lilies, a garland of roses,
   A little straw hat to set off the blue ribbons
   That tie up my bonny brown hair.

98
Oh, How Lovely Is the Evening

Moderately fast

Traditional English Round

① Oh, how love-ly is the eve-ning, is the eve-ning;

② When the bells are sweet-ly ring-ing, sweet-ly ring-ing;

③ Ding, dong, ding; ding, dong, ding.

99
Oh, Mary, Don't You Weep

Additional lyrics by J.F.L.

American Negro Spiritual

Moderately

Chorus

Oh, Mar-y, don't you weep, don't you mourn; Oh, Mar-y, don't you weep, don't you mourn; Phar-aoh's ar-my got drown-ded,

Oh, Mar-y don't you weep. If I could I sure-ly would Stand on the rock where Mos-es stood.

Phar-aoh's ar-my got drown-ded, Oh, Mar-y, don't you weep.

2. Wonder what Satan's grumblin' 'bout,
   Chained in Hell an' he can't git out.
   Pharaoh's army got drownded,
   Oh, Mary, don't you weep.

Continue, as above:

3. Ol' Satan's mad an' I am glad,
   He missed that soul he thought he had.

4. Brother, better mind how you walk on the cross,
   Foot might slip and your soul get lost.

5. One of these nights about twelve o'clock,
   This old world's goin' to reel and rock.

6. I went down in the valley to pray,
   My soul got joy and I stayed all day.

7. Now don't you believe the Bible ain't true,
   'Cause you'll be sorry if you do.

8. That primrose path is wide and fair,
   Many a soul's done perished there.

100

Oh, Mister Moon

Traditional, American

101

101
Oh, No, John

English Folk Song

Women:

2. My father was a Spanish captain,
   Went to sea a month ago;
   First he kissed me, then he left me;
   Told me always answer no. (*Chorus*)

Men:

3. Oh, madam, in your face is beauty,
   On your lips red roses' glow,
   Will you take me for your lover?
   Madam, answer yes or no. (*Chorus*)

Men:

4. Oh, madam, I will give you jewels,
   I will make you rich and free,
   I will give you silken dresses;
   Madam, will you marry me? (*Chorus*)

Men:

5. Oh, madam, since you are so cruel,
   And since you do scorn me so,
   If I may not be your lover,
   Madam, will you let me go? (*Chorus*)

Men:

6. Then I will stay with you forever,
   If you will not be unkind,
   Madam, I have vowed to love you,
   Would you have me change my mind? (*Chorus*)

Men:

7. Oh, hark, I hear the church bells ringing,
   Will you come and be my wife?
   Or, dear madam, have you settled
   To live single all your life? (*Chorus*)

102
Oh, Won't You Sit Down?

American Negro Spiritual

Moderately and rhythmically

Chorus

Oh, won't you sit down? Lord, I can't sit down. Oh, won't you sit down? Lord, I can't sit down. Oh, won't you sit down? Lord, I can't sit down, 'Cause I just got to heav-en, Got to look a - round.

Verse

Who's that yon-der dressed in red? Must be the chil-dren that Mo-ses led.

Who's that yon-der dressed in white? Must be the chil-dren of the Is-rael-ite.

2. Who's that yonder dressed in blue?
   Must be the children that are comin' through.
   Who's that yonder dressed in black?
   Must be the hypocrites a-turnin' back.

103
The Old Ark's A-Moverin'

American Negro Spiritual

Moderately brisk and rhythmic

Chorus

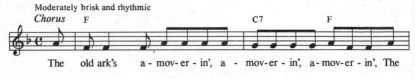

The old ark's a-mov-er-in', a-mov-er-in', a-mov-er-in', The

old ark's a-mov-in' by the Spir-it of God! The old ark's a-mov-er-in', a-

mov-er-in', a-mov-er-in', The old ark's a-mov-in' and I thank God.

Verse

Call

Response

How man-y days did the wa-ter fall? For-ty days and nights in all.

Call

Response

Old ark she rocked, Old ark she rocked, Old ark she land-ed on the moun-tain top.

2. Ham, Shem, and Japheth were settin' one day,
Talkin' on the upper deck and lookin' at the bay;
While they were disputin' 'bout this and that,
The ark done bump on Ararat.

3. See that sister all dressed so fine.
She ain't got Jesus on her mind.
See that brother all dressed so gay?
Death's gonna come and carry him away.

4. See that sister there comin' so slow?
   She wants to go to heaven 'fore the heaven door close.
   Ain't but one-a thing on my mind,
   My sister's gone to heaven an'-a lef'-a me behin'.

104
On the First Thanksgiving Day

Traditional, American

Moderately slow

On the first Thanks-giv - ing Day,   Pil-grims went to   church to pray,

Thanked the Lord for   sun   and rain,   Thanked him for the   fields of grain.

Now Thanks-giv - ing   comes a - gain: Praise   the Lord as   they did then.

Thank him for   the   sun and rain,   Thank him for the   fields of grain.

105
On Top of Old Smoky

American Folk Song

On top of old Smok - y, All cov - ered with snow,_____

_____ I lost my true lov - er By court-in' too slow._____

2. Now, courting's a pleasure,
   Parting is grief;
   But a false-hearted lover
   Is worse than a thief.

3. A thief he will rob you
   And take all you have;
   But a false-hearted lover
   Will lead you to the grave.

4. The grave will decay you
   And turn you to dust,
   There ain't one in a million
   A poor girl (boy) can trust.

5. They'll hug you and kiss you
   And tell you more lies
   Than the crossties on railroads
   Or the stars in the skies.

6. They'll tell you they love you
   To give your heart ease;
   But the minute your back's turned,
   They'll court who they please.

7. I'll go back to old Smoky,
   Old Smoky so high,
   Where the wild birds and turtledoves
   Can hear my sad cry.

8. Bury me on old Smoky,
   Old Smoky so high,
   Where the wild birds in heaven
   Can hear my sad cry.

9. On top of old Smoky,
   All covered with snow,
   I lost my true lover
   By courtin' too slow.

106
Once There Were Three Fishermen

American Folk Song

Once there were three fish - er - men,

Once there were three fish- er - men.   Fish-er, fish-er, men, men, men.

Fish-er, fish-er, men, men, men,   Once there were three fish- er - men.

2. The first one's name was Abraham,
   The first one's name was Abraham,
   Abra, Abra, ham, ham, ham,
   Abra, Abra, ham, ham, ham,
   The first one's name was Abraham.

Continue, as above:

3. The second one's name was Isaac.
   Isey, Isey, ack, ack, ack.

4. The third one's name was Jacob.
   Jakey, Jakey, cub, cub, cub.

5. They all sailed up to Jericho.
   Jerry, Jerry, cho, cho, cho.

6. Instead of going to Amsterdam.
   Amster, Amster, sh, sh, sh.

7. Oh, do not say that naughty word.
   Naughty, naughty, word, word, word.

107
One More River to Cross

American Student Song

Lively

Old No-ah, he built him-self an ark, There's one more riv-er to cross,— He built it out of hick-o-ry bark, There's one more riv-er to cross.— **Chorus** There's one more riv-er,— And that's the riv-er of Jor-dan:— There's one more riv-er,— Just one more riv-er to cross.—

2. He went to work to load his stock,
   There's one more river to cross.
   He anchored the ark with a great big rock,
   There's one more river to cross.

Chorus.

Continue, as above:

3. The animals went in one by one,
   The elephant with a big bass drum.

4. The animals went in two by two,
   The rhinoceros and the kangaroo.

5. The animals went in three by three,
   The bear, the flea, and the bumblebee.

6. The animals went in four by four,
   Noah got mad and hollered for more.

7. The animals went in five by five,
   Shem, Ham, and Japhet, and their wives.

8. When Noah found he had no sail,
He just ran up his old shirttail.

9. Now, Mrs. Noah, she got drunk,
She kicked the old sailor out of his bunk,

10. Now you may think there's another verse,
Well, there ain't!

108
Over the River and Through the Woods

Traditional, American

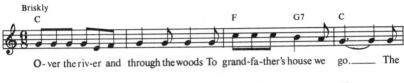

O-ver the riv-er and through the woods To grand-fa-ther's house we go.___ The

horse knows the way To car-ry the sleigh Thro'the white and drift-ed snow.___

O-ver the riv-er and through the woods,Oh how the wind does blow!___ It

stings your nose And bites your toes, As o-ver the ground we go.___

2. Over the river and through the woods,
   Trot fast, my dapple gray!
      Spring over the ground
      Like a hunting hound,
   For this is Thanksgiving Day!
   Over the river and through the wood,
   Now grandmother's face I spy!
      Hurrah for the fun!
      Is the pudding done?
   Hurrah for the pumpkin pie!

109
Paper of Pins

Anglo-American Folk Song

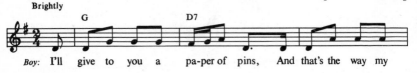

Brightly

Boy: I'll give to you a pa-per of pins, And that's the way my

love be-gins, If you will mar-ry me, me, me, If you will mar-ry me.

Girl:
2. I'll not accept your paper of pins,
   If that's the way your love begins,
   And I'll not marry you, you, you,
   For I'll not marry you.

Boy:
3. I'll give to you a dress of red
   All bound round with golden thread,
   If you will marry me, me, me,
   If you will marry me.

Girl:
4. I'll not accept your dress of red
   All bound round with golden thread,
   And I'll not marry you, you, you,
   For I'll not marry you.

Boy:
5. I'll give to you a little dog
   To take with you abroad, abroad.
   (*Refrain*)

Girl:
6. I'll not accept your little dog
   To take with me abroad, abroad.
   (*Refrain*)

Boy:
7. I'll give to you a dappled horse
   So you can ride from cross to cross.
   (*Refrain*)

Girl:
8. I'll not accept your dappled horse
   And I'll not ride from cross to cross.
   (*Refrain*)

Boy:
9. I'll give to you the keys to my chest
   And all the money that I possess,
   If you will marry me, me, me,
   If you will marry me.

Girl:
10. Oh, yes, I'll take the keys to your chest
    And all the money that you possess,
    And I will marry you, you, you,
    And I will marry you.

Boy:
11. Oh, now I see that money is all,
    And your love is nothing at all,
    So I won't marry you, you, you,
    No, I won't marry you.

12. Then I shall be an old maid,
    And take a chair and sit in the shade,
    And I will marry none at all,
    I'll marry none at all.

    *If you want the boy to win the
    girl, use this ending:*

Boy:

9A. I'll give to you the gift of my heart,
    That we may love and never part,
    And I will marry you, you, you,
    Oh, I will marry you.

Girl:

10A. Oh, I'll accept the gift of your heart,
    And we shall love and never part.
    Yes, I will marry you, you, you,
    Oh, I will marry you.

    Or she can marry someone else:

Boy:

11A. Well, you love coffee and I love tea;
    You love money, but you don't love me.
    I won't marry you, you, you,
    No, I won't marry you.

Girl:

12A. Yes, I love coffee and I hate tea;
    Without your money you're not for me;
    And I will marry someone else,
    I'll marry someone else.

110

Pick a Bale of Cotton

American Negro Folk Song

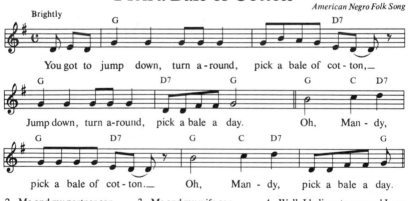

You got to jump down, turn a - round, pick a bale of cot - ton,—
Jump down, turn a-round, pick a bale a day. Oh, Man - dy,
pick a bale of cot - ton.— Oh, Man - dy, pick a bale a day.

2. Me and my partner can
   Pick a bale of cotton,
   Me and my partner can
   Pick a bale a day. (*Chorus*)

3. Me and my wife can
   Pick a bale of cotton,
   Me and my wife can
   Pick a bale a day. (*Chorus*)
   Extra verses:

4. Well, I believe to my soul I can
   Pick a bale of cotton,
   Believe to my soul I can
   Pick a bale a day. (*Chorus*)

I went down the road to, etc.

Gonna fill my jeans if I, etc.

Knew a little woman could, etc.

You can't go home till you, etc.

111
A Poor Wayfaring Stranger

American White Spiritual

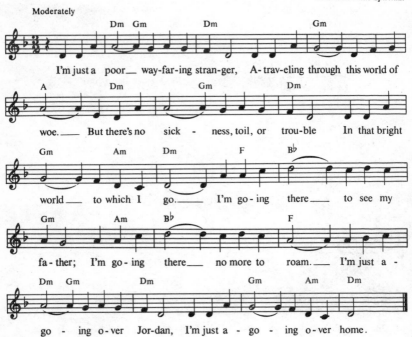

I'm just a poor__ way-far-ing stran-ger, A-trav-eling through this world of woe.__ But there's no sick - ness, toil, or trou-ble In that bright world__ to which I go.__ I'm go-ing there__ to see my fa-ther; I'm go-ing there__ no more to roam.__ I'm just a - go - ing o-ver Jor-dan, I'm just a - go - ing o-ver home.

112
Putting on the Style

American Popular Song

Two wheels 'round a cor-ner, Driv-ing like he's mad;

(Melody in lower notes)

Young man in an au-to He bor-rowed from his dad; He
honks his horn so loud-ly To see his girl friend smile;
But she knows he's on - ly Put-ting on the style.

Chorus

Put-ting on the ag-o-ny, Put-ting on the style,
That's what ev-'ry-bod-y's Do-ing all the while. And
as I look a-round me It makes me want to smile, To
see so man-y peo-ple Put-ting on the style.

2. Sweet sixteen and goes to church
   Just to see the boys;
   See her laugh and giggle
   At every little noise.
   She turns her head a little
   And stands that way awhile,
   But everybody knows she's only
   Putting on the style. (*Chorus*)

3. Young man home from college
   Makes a big display
   With a giant jawbreaker
   That he can hardly say;
   It can't be found in Webster
   And won't be for awhile,
   But everybody knows he's only
   Putting on the style. (*Chorus*)

113

113
The Riddle Song

English Folk Song

Slowly

I gave my love a cher-ry that has no stone, I gave my love a chick-en that has no bone, I gave my love a ring that has no end, I gave my love a ba-by that's no cry-in'.

2. How can there be a cherry that has no stone?
   How can there be a chicken that has no bone?
   How can there be a ring that has no end?
   How can there be a baby that's no cryin'?

3. A cherry when it's bloomin', it has no stone;
   A chicken when it's pippin', it has no bone;
   A ring when it's rollin', it has no end;
   A baby when it's sleepin', it's no cryin'.

114
Rise and Shine

American Negro Folk Song
(Adapted)

Brightly

C

1.   Rise   and   shine,   and give God   the   glo - ry, glo - ry,
(2. The) Lord   said, "No-ah,   there's gon-na be   a   flood-y, flood-y,
(3. So) No-ah   he   went out   and   he   built   an   ark- y, ark- y,
(4. The) an-i-mals, they   came,   and went in __   by   two-sy, two-sy,
(5. It) rained   and rained   for for__   ty   day-sy, day-sy,

G7

Rise__   and   shine __   and   give God __ the   glo - ry, glo - ry,
Lord__   said: "No - ah,   there's   gon - na be   a   flood- y, flood- y,
No - ah   he   went out   and   he   built__   an   ark- y, ark - y,
An-imals,   they   came,   and   went in ____   by   two- sy, two - sy,
Rained   and   rained   __   for for - ty   day - sy, day - sy,

C   **C7**   **F**   **C**

Rise   and   shine   and   give God the   glo - ry, glo - ry,
Get   your   chil - dren   out   of   the   mud - dy, mud-dy,
Made   it   out   of   hick - o - ry   bark - y, bark - y,
El - e - phants   and   kan - ga - roo - sy, roo - sy,
Drove   those   an - imals   near - ly   cra - zy, cra - zy,

C   **G7**   **C**   **1.2.3.4.**   *last time*

Chil - dren   of   the   Lord. _____   2. The
                                                   3. So
                                                   4. The
                                                   5. It

115
The Rock Island Line

American Folk Song

Fast
Chorus

I say the Rock Is-land Line___ is a might-y good road,___ I say the Rock Is-land Line___ is the road to ride. Oh, the Rock Is-land Line___ is a might-y good road,___ If you want to ride it, got to ride it, like you're fly-in', Buy your tick-et at the sta-tion on the Rock Is-land Line.

Fine

Verse

I may be right and I may be wrong, I know you're gon-na miss me when I___ have gone.___

D.C.

2. A, B, C, Double X, Y, Z,
   Cat's in the cupboard, but he can't see me.

3. Jesus died to save our sins,
   Glory be to God, we're gonna need him again.

116
Roll, Jordan, Roll

American Negro Spiritual

Majestically

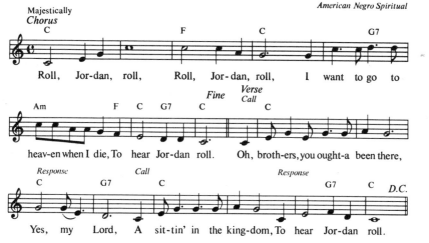

Roll, Jor-dan, roll, Roll, Jor-dan, roll, I want to go to heav-en when I die, To hear Jor-dan roll. Oh, broth-ers, you ought-a been there, Yes, my Lord, A sit-tin' in the king-dom, To hear Jor-dan roll.

2. Oh, preacher, you oughta been there,
   Yes, my Lord,
   A-sitting' in the Kingdom
   To hear Jordan roll.

Continue, as above:

3. Oh, sinner, you oughta been there.

4. Oh, mourner, you oughta been there.

5. Oh, seekers, you oughta been there.

6. Oh, mothers, you oughta been there.

7. Oh, children, you oughta been there.

117
Row, Row, Row Your Boat

Traditional American Round

Lively

Row, row, row your boat, Gen - tly down the stream. Mer-ri-ly, mer-ri-ly, mer-ri-ly, mer-ri-ly, Life is but a dream.

118
Scotland's Burning

Traditional British Round

Scot-land's burn-ing, Scot-land's burn-ing, Look out! Look out!

Fire! Fire! Fire! Fire! Pour on wa-ter, Pour on wa-ter.

119
The Seven Joys of Mary

Traditional English Carol
Arr. by John Stainer

The first good joy that Ma-ry had, It was the joy of one;___ To

see the bless-ed Je-sus Christ, When he was first her Son,___ When

he was first her Son, Good Lord, And hap-py may we be;___ Praise

Fa-ther, Son, and Ho-ly Ghost To all e-ter-ni-ty.

2. The next good joy that Mary had,
   It was the joy of two;
   To see her own Son Jesus Christ,
   Making the lame to go,
   Making the lame to go, Good Lord,
   And happy may we be;
   Praise Father, Son, and Holy Ghost
   To all eternity.

3. The next good joy that Mary had,
   It was the joy of three;
   To see her own Son Jesus Christ,
   Making the blind to see,
   Making the blind to see, Good Lord,
   And happy may we be;
   Praise Father, Son, and Holy Ghost
   To all eternity.

4. The next good joy that Mary had,
   It was the joy of four;
   To see her own Son Jesus Christ,
   Reading the Bible o'er.
   Reading the Bible o'er, Good Lord,
   And happy may we be;
   Praise Father, Son, and Holy Ghost
   To all eternity.

5. The next good joy that May had,
   It was the joy of five;
   To see her own Son Jesus Christ,
   Raising the dead to life.
   Raising the dead to life, Good Lord,
   And happy may we be;
   Praise Father, Son, and Holy Ghost
   To all eternity.

6. The next good joy that Mary had,
   It was the joy of six;
   To see her own Son Jesus Christ
   Upon the Crucifix.
   Upon the Crucifix, Good Lord,
   And happy may we be;
   Praise Father, Son, and Holy Ghost
   To all eternity.

7. The next good joy that Mary had,
   It was the joy of seven;
   To see her own Son Jesus Christ
   Ascending into heaven.
   Ascending into heaven, Good Lord,
   And happy may we be;
   Praise Father, Son, and Holy Ghost
   To all eternity.

120

She'll Be Coming 'Round the Mountain

American Folk Song

She'll be com-ing 'round the moun-tain when she comes.___

___ She'll be com-ing 'round the moun-tain when she comes.___

___ She'll be com-ing 'round the moun-tain, She'll be com-ing 'round the

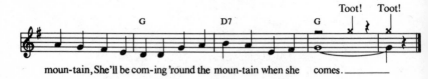

moun-tain, She'll be com-ing 'round the moun-tain when she comes.___

2. She'll be driving six white horses when she comes. (Whoa, back!)
   She'll be driving six white horses when she comes. (Whoa, back!)
   She'll be driving six white horses,
   She'll be driving six white horses,
   She'll be driving six white horses when she comes. (Whoa, back!)

   Continue, as above:

3. Oh, we'll all go out to meet her when she comes. (Hi, babe!)
4. Oh, we'll all have chicken and dumplings when she comes. (Yum! yum!)

121
Shenandoah

Revised by J.F.L.

American Sea Chantey

Slowly

Oh, Shen-an-doah,— I long to see you, A - way,——— you roll-ing

riv- er.— Oh, Shen-an-doah,— I long to see you. A -

way, we're bound a - way——— 'Cross the wide Mis - sou - ri.

2. Oh, Shenandoah's my native valley,
   Away, you rolling river.
   Oh, Shenandoah's my native valley.
   Away, we're bound away
   'Cross the wide Missouri.

Continue, as above:

3. Oh, Shenandoah, it's far I wander.

4. Oh, Shenandoah has rushing waters.

5. Oh, Shenandoah, I long to hear you.

6. Oh, Shenandoah, I love your daughter.

7. Oh, Shenandoah, I'll never leave you.

8. Oh, Shenandoah, I'll never grieve you.

122
The Sidewalks of New York

Words and Music by
Charles B. Lawlor and James W. Blake

East side, west side, all a-round the town, ___ The tots sang "Ring-a-Ros-ie," "Lon-don bridge is fall-ing down." ___ Boys and girls to-geth-er, ___ Me and Ma-mie O'-Rourk, ___ Tripped the light__ fan-tas-tic On the side-walks of New York. ___

123
Silent Night

Joseph Mohr
Trans. by John F. Young and others

Franz Gruber

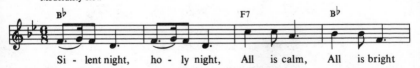

Si - lent night, ho - ly night, All is calm, All is bright

Round yon vir - gin moth-er and child. Ho - ly in - fant so ten-der and mild,

Sleep in heav-en-ly peace,__ sleep in heav-en-ly peace.__

2. Silent night, holy night,
   Shepherds quake at the sight,
   Glories stream from heaven afar,
   Heavenly hosts sing Alleluiah;
   Christ the Savior is born!
   Christ the Savior is born!

3. Silent night, holy night,
   Son of God, love's pure light
   Radiant beams from thy holy face,
   With the dawn of redeeming grace,
   Jesus, Lord, at thy birth,
   Jesus, Lord, at thy birth,

German words:

1. Stille nacht, heilige nacht,
   Alles schlaft, einsam wacht
   Nur das traute hochheilige Paar,
   Holder Knabe im lockigen Haar,
   Schlaf in himmlischer Ruh,
   Schlaf in himmlischer Ruh,

2. Stille Nacht, heilige Nacht!
   Hirten erst kundgemacht
   Durch der Engel Halleluja
   Tönt es laut von fern und nah:
   Christ, der Retter, ist da,
   Christ, der Retter, ist da!

3. Stille Nacht, heilige Nacht!
   Gottes Sohn, o wie lacht
   Lieb' aus deinem göttlichen Mund,
   Da uns schlagt die rettende Stund',
   Christ, in deiner Geburt,
   Christ, in deiner Geburt.

124
Sing Your Way Home

Traditional, American

Brightly

Sing your way home at the close of the day.

Sing your way home, drive the shad - ows a - way.

Smile ev - ery mile for wher - ev - er you roam, It will bright-en your

road, It will light-en your load, If you sing your way home.

125
Sinner Man

American Folk Hymn

Oh,   sin - ner man,   where you gon - na   run   to?

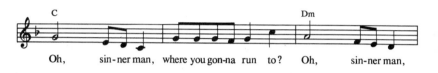

Oh,   sin-ner man,   where you gon-na run   to?   Oh,   sin-ner man,

where you gon - na   run   to?   All   on   that   day?

2. Run to the rock, the rock was a-melting, (*3 times*)
   All on that day.

3. Run to the sea, the sea was a-boiling, (*3 times*)
   All on that day.

4. Run to the moon, the moon was a-bleeding, (*3 times*)
   All on that day.

5. Run to the Lord, "Lord, won't you hide me?" (*3 times*)
   All on that day.

6. Run to the Devil, Devil was a-waiting. (*3 times*)
   All on that day.

7. Oh, sinner man, you oughta been a-praying, (*3 times*)
   All on that day.

126
Sipping Cider Through a Straw

Traditional American

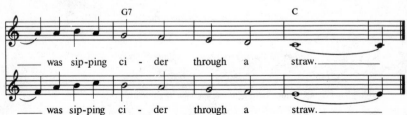

2. I told that girl I didn't see how
   She sipped that cider through a straw.
   I told that girl I didn't see how
   She sipped that cider through a straw.

   Continue, as above:

4. And now and then the straw would slip,
   And I'd sip cider from her lip.

3. Then cheek to cheek, and jaw to jaw,
   We sipped that cider through a straw.

5. And now I've got a mother-in-law
   From sipping cider through a straw.

127
Six Little Ducks

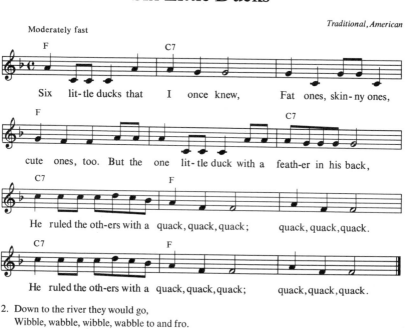

Moderately fast

Traditional, American

Six lit-tle ducks that I once knew, Fat ones, skin-ny ones,

cute ones, too. But the one lit-tle duck with a feath-er in his back,

He ruled the oth-ers with a quack, quack, quack; quack, quack, quack.

He ruled the oth-ers with a quack, quack, quack; quack, quack, quack.

2. Down to the river they would go,
   Wibble, wabble, wibble, wabble to and fro.
   But the one little duck with a feather in his back,
   He ruled the others with a slap, slap, slap.
   He ruled the others with a slap, slap, slap.

3. Home from the river they would come,
   Wibble, wabble, wibble, wabble, ho-um-hum.
   But the one little duck with a feather in his back,
   He led the others with a quack, quack, quack.
   He led the others with a quack, quack, quack.

128
The Sloop John B.

Bahamian Folk Song

Oh, we came on the Sloop John B. My grand-fa-ther and me. 'Round Nas-sau town we did roam. Drink-in' all night We got in a fight, Oh, I feel so break-up, I want-a go home.

Chorus (same tune as verse):

So, hoist up the John B. sails, see how the mainsail's set,
Send for the cap'n ashore, lemme go home!
Lemme go home! Lemme go home!
I feel so break-up, I want to go home.

2. The first mate he got drunk, break up the people's trunk,
   Constable come aboard and take him away,
   Mr. Johnstone, please let me alone,
   I feel so break-up, I want to go home.

3. The poor cook he got fits, throw 'way all the grits,
   Then he took and eat up all o' my corn,
   Lemme go home, I want to go home,
   This is the worst trip, since I been born!

129
Soldier, Soldier, Will You Marry Me ?

Anglo-American Folk Song

"Oh, sol-dier, sol-dier, will you mar-ry me with your fife and drum?" "Oh,

no, oh no," the sol-dier re-plied, "I have no shoes to put on."

2. Away she flew to the cobbler's shop.
   Bought him the very best pair.
   Came right back and he put them on,
   And she said, "Now there you are. So . . .

3. "Soldier, soldier, will you marry me
   With your fife and drum?"
   "Oh no, oh no," the soldier replied,
   "I have no hat to put on."

4. Away she flew to the hatter's shop,
   Got him the very best hat.
   Came right back and he put it on,
   And she said, "Now look at that. So . . .

5. "Soldier, soldier, will you marry me
   With your fife and drum?"
   "Oh no, oh no," the soldier replied,
   "I have no suit to put on."

6. Away she flew to the tailor's shop,
   Got him the very best suit.
   Came right back and he put it on,
   And she said, "Now that's to boot. So . . .

7. "Soldier, soldier, will you marry me
   With your fife and drum?"
   "Oh no, oh no," the soldier replied,
   "I've a wife and children at home!"

130
Standing in the Need of Prayer

American Negro Spiritual

Moderately

Verse

Call

Ain't my broth-er or my sis-ter, but it's me, oh Lord,

Response (Melody in upper notes)

stand-ing in the need of prayer.

Call

Ain't my broth-er or my sis-ter, but it's

Response (Melody in upper notes)

Fine

me, oh Lord, stand-ing in the need of prayer.

Chorus

Call

Response

Call

It's me (it's me), it's me, oh Lord,

Response

Stand-ing in the need of prayer.

Call

Response *Call*

It's me (it's me), it's

Response

D.C.

me, oh Lord, Stand-ing in the need of prayer.

2. Ain't my father or my mother, but it's me, oh Lord,
   Standing in the need of prayer.
   Ain't my father or my mother, but it's me, oh Lord,
   Standing in the need of prayer.   *Continue, as above:*

   Chorus

   3. Ain't the preacher or the deacon, but it's me, oh Lord.

   4. Ain't my neighbor or a stranger, but it's me, oh Lord.

131
The Star-Spangled Banner

Francis Scott Key

John Stafford Smith (?)

132
Steal Away

American Negro Spiritual

Moderately slow

Chorus

Steal a-way, steal a-way, Steal a-way to Je - sus.

Steal a-way, steal a-way home, I ain't got long to stay here.

Verse

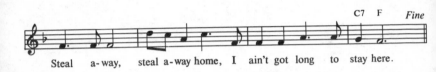

My Lord calls me; He calls me by the thun-der, The

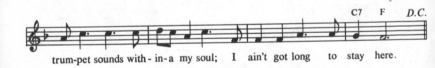

trum-pet sounds with-in-a my soul; I ain't got long to stay here.

2. Green trees a-bending,
   Poor sinner stands a-trembling.
   The trumpet sounds with-in-a my soul,
   I ain't got long to stay here.

Continue, as above:

3. My Lord calls me,
   He calls me by the lightning.

4. Tombstones are bursting,
   Poor sinners stand trembling.

133
Stodola Pumpa

Verse by Robert E. Nye
Moderately slow

Czechoslovakian Folk Song

Verse

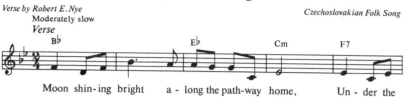

Moon shin-ing bright a - long the path-way home, Un - der the

trees, we walk there all a - lone. Moon shin-ing bright a -

long the path-way home, Un - der the trees we walk there all a - lone. Hey!

Fast
Chorus

Sto-do-la, sto-do-la, sto-do-la, pum-pa, Sto-do-la pum-pa, Sto-do-la pum-pa.

Sto-do-la, sto-do-la, sto-do-la, pum-pa, Sto-do-la, pum-pa, pum, pum, pum!

134
The Streets of Laredo

Anglo-American Ballad

Moderately slow

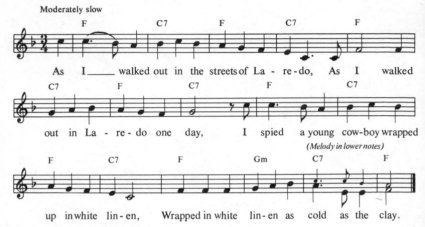

As I____ walked out in the streets of La - re - do, As I walked out in La - re - do one day, I spied a young cow-boy wrapped

(Melody in lower notes)

up in white lin - en, Wrapped in white lin - en as cold as the clay.

2. "I see by your outfit that you are a cowboy"—
These words he did say as I boldly stepped by,
"Come sit down beside me and hear my sad story;
I was shot in the breast and I know I must die.

3. "It was once in the saddle I used to go dashing,
It was once in the saddle I used to go gay;
First to the dram-house and then to the card-house;
Got shot in the breast; I am dying today.

4. "Get six jolly cowboys to carry my coffin;
Get six pretty maidens to carry my pall;
Put bunches of roses all over my coffin,
Roses to deaden the clods as they fall.

5. "Oh, beat the drum slowly and play the fife lowly.
Play the dead march as you carry me along;
Take me to the green valley and lay the sod o'er me.
For I'm a young cowboy and I know I've done wrong.

6. "Go gather around you a crowd of young cowboys
And tell them the story of this, my sad fate,
Tell one and the other before they go further
To stop their wild roving before it's too late.

7. "Go fetch me a cup, a cup of cold water,
To cool my parched lips," the cowboy then said;
Before I returned, the spirit had left him
And gone to its Maker—the cowboy was dead.

135
Sur le Pont d'Avignon

French Folk Song

Moderately fast and light

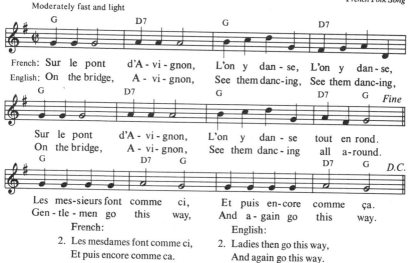

French: Sur le pont d'A - vi - gnon, L'on y dan - se, L'on y dan - se,
English: On the bridge, A - vi - gnon, See them danc-ing, See them danc-ing,

Sur le pont d'A - vi - gnon, L'on y dan - se tout en rond.
On the bridge, A - vi - gnon, See them danc - ing all a - round.

Les mes-sieurs font comme ci, Et puis en-core comme ça.
Gen - tle - men go this way, And a - gain go this way.

French:
2. Les mesdames font comme ci,
   Et puis encore comme ca.

English:
2. Ladies then go this way,
   And again go this way.

136
Sweetly Sings the Donkey

Traditional American Round

Brightly

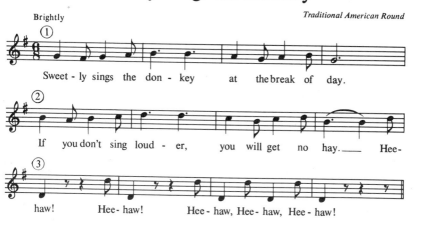

① Sweet - ly sings the don - key at the break of day.

② If you don't sing loud - er, you will get no hay. ___ Hee-

③ haw! Hee- haw! Hee - haw, Hee- haw, Hee - haw!

137
Swing Low, Sweet Chariot

American Negro Spiritual

Moderately slow
Chorus

Swing low, sweet char - i - ot,— Com-in' for to car-ry me home!

(Melody in lower notes)   *Fine*

Swing low, sweet char - i - ot,— Com-in' for to car-ry me home.

Verse
Call

I looked o - ver Jor-dan and what did I see,—

Response   Call

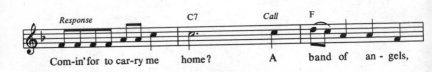

Com-in' for to car-ry me home?   A band of an - gels,

Response
(Melody in lower notes)   *D.C.*

com-in' af - ter me,—   Com-in' for to car-ry me home!

2. If you get there before I do,
   Comin' for to carry me home!
   Tell all my friends I'm coming, too,
   Comin' for to carry me home!

Continue, as above:

3. The brightest day that ever I saw,
   When Jesus washed my sins away.

4. I'm sometimes up an' sometimes down,
   But still my soul feels heavenly boun'.

5. I never went to heaven, but I been told
   The streets in heaven are paved with gold.

138
Taps

Traditional, American

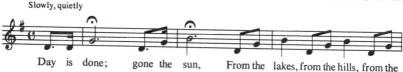

Slowly, quietly

Day is done; gone the sun, From the lakes, from the hills, from the

sky. All is well, safe-ly rest; God is nigh.

2. Fading light dims the sight,
   And a star lights the sky, gleaming bright;
   From afar, drawing nigh,
   Falls the night.

3. Thanks and praise for our days
   'Neath the sun, 'neath the stars, 'neath the sky;
   As we go, this we know:
   God is nigh.

139
Tell Me Why

Adapted by J.F.L.

Traditional, American
Adapted by J.F.L.

Please tell — me why — the stars do shine.

Tell — me why — the i - vy twines, Then

tell — me why — the sky is blue,

And I will tell you why I — love you.

2. Because God made the stars to shine,
   Because God made the ivy twine,
   Because God made the sky so blue,
   Because God made you so sweet and true.

3. I know it's true that God above,
   He wanted someone for me to love.
   And he chose you from all the rest,
   Because he knew, dear, I'd love you the best.

140
Ten Green Bottles

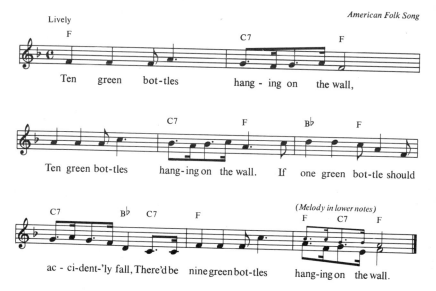

American Folk Song

Lively

Ten green bot-tles hang-ing on the wall,
Ten green bot-tles hang-ing on the wall. If one green bot-tle should
ac-ci-dent-'ly fall, There'd be nine green bot-tles hang-ing on the wall.

2. Nine green bottles hanging on the wall,
   Nine green bottles hanging on the wall.
   If one green bottle should accidentally fall,
   There'd be eight green bottles hanging on the wall.

   *Continue with eight, then seven, and so on, until there
   are no green bottles left on the wall.*

141
There Was an Old Woman

American Folk Song

Moderately

G
1. There was an old wo-man who swal-lowed a fly.

Am   D7   G
I don't know why she swal-lowed a fly, Per-haps she'll die.

G   Am
2. There was an old wo-man who swal-lowed a spi-der, who wrig-gled and jig-gled and

D7   G
tic-kled in-side her. She swal-lowed the spi-der to catch the fly. And

Am   D7   G
I don't know why she swal-lowed a fly. Per-haps she'll die.

G   Guitar tacet
3. There was an old wo-man who swal-lowed a bird. *(Spoken)* How ab-surd! To

D7   G
swal-low a bird. She swal-lowed the bird to catch the spi-der that

Am   D7   G
wrig-gled and jig-gled and tic-kled in-side her. She swal-lowed the spi-der to

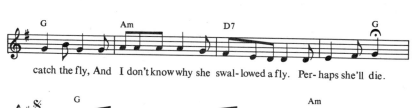

catch the fly, And I don't know why she swal-lowed a fly. Per-haps she'll die.

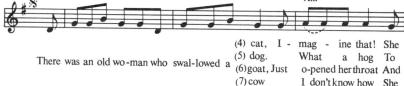

There was an old wo-man who swal-lowed a

(4) cat, I - mag - ine that! She
(5) dog. What a hog To
(6) goat, Just o-pened her throat And
(7) cow I don't know how She

(Repeat as need to complete accumulation)

swal-lowed a cat. She swal-lowed the cat to catch the bird,
swal-low a dog. She swal-lowed the dog to catch the cat,
swal-lowed a goat. She swal-lowed the goat to catch the dog, She
swal-lowed a cow. She swal-lowed the cow to catch the goat,

swal-lowed the bird to catch the spi-der that wrig-gled and jig-gled and

tic-kled in-side her. She swal-lowed the spi-der to catch the fly. And

I don't know why she swal-lowed a fly. Per - haps she'll die.

Coda

8. There was an old wo-man who swal-lowed a horse. She died, of course!

141

142
There's a Song in the Air

Josiah G. Holland   *Karl P. Harrington*

There's a song in the air! There's a star in the sky! There's a mother's deep prayer, And a baby's low cry! And the star rains its fire while the beautiful sing, For the manger of Bethlehem cradles a King!

2. There's a tumult of joy
   O'er the wonderful birth,
   For the virgin's sweet boy
   Is the Lord of the earth.
   Ay! the star rains its fire while the beautiful sing,
   For the manger of Bethlehem cradles a King!

3. In the light of that star
   Lie the ages impearled,
   And that song from afar
   Has swept over the world.
   Every hearth is aflame, and the beautiful sing
   In the homes of the nations that Jesus is King!

4. We rejoice in the light,
   And we echo the song
   That comes down through the night
   From the heavenly throng.
   Ay! we shout to the lovely evangel they bring,
   And we greet in his cradle our Savior and King!

143

This Old Man

Lively

Traditional, English

This old man, he played one, He played knick knack on my thumb; knick knack pad-dy whack, Give a dog a bone, This old man came roll - ing home.

2. This old man, he played two,
   He played knick knack on my shoe.
   Knick knack, paddy whack, give a dog a bone,
   This old man came rolling home.

   Continue, as above:

3. This old man, he played three,
   He played knick knack on my knee.

4. This old man, he played four,
   He played knick knack on my door;

5. This old man, he played five,
   He played knick knack on my hive;

6. This old man, he played six,
   He played knick knack on my sticks;

7. This old man, he played seven
   He played knick knack up in heaven;

8. This old man, he played eight,
   He played knick knack on my pate;

9. This old man, he played nine,
   He played knick knack on my spine,

10. This old man, he played ten,
    He played knick knack once again;
    Knick knack, paddy whack, give a dog a bone,
    Now we'll all go running home.

144
This Train

American Negro Spiritual

2. This train don't carry no gamblers, this train,
   This train don't carry no gamblers, this train,
   This train don't carry no gamblers,
   No hypocrites, no midnight ramblers,
   This train is bound for glory, this train.

   Continue, as above:

3. This train is built for speed now, *etc*.
   Fastest train you ever did see,
   This train is bound for glory, this train.

4. This train don't carry no liars, *etc*.
   No hypocrites and no high flyers,
   This train is bound for glory, this train.

5. This train don't carry no rustlers, *etc*.
   Sidestreet walkers, two-bit hustlers.
   This train is bound for glory, this train.

145
Three Blind Mice

Traditional English Round

Three blind mice, three blind mice,

See how they run, see how they run.____ They

all ran af-ter the far-mer's wife. She cut off their tales with a carv-ing knife. Did you

ev - er see such a sight in your life, as three blind mice.

146
Tom Dooley

American Ballad

Moderately
Chorus

Hang down your head, Tom Doo - ley,

Hang down your head and cry, Hang down your head, Tom

Doo - ley, Poor boy, you're bound to die.

1. I met her on the hilltop.
   There I took her life.
   I met her on the hilltop,
   And stabbed her with my knife.

2. Tonight I'll pick my banjo,
   I'll pick it on my knee.
   Tomorrow I'll be hangin'
   From a white oak tree.

3. This time tomorrow,
   Reckon where I'll be.
   This time tomorrow,
   I'll be in eternity.

4. Had my trial in Wilkesboro.
   What do you think they done?
   Bound me over to Statesville,
   And that's where I'll be hung.

5. Daddy, oh my Daddy,
   What shall I do?
   I've lost all my money,
   And killed poor Laury, too.

6. Mother, oh dear Mother,
   Don't you weep and cry.
   I've killed poor Laury Foster,
   You know I'm bound to die.

7. Now, what my Mother told me
   Is about to come to pass:
   That drinkin' and the women
   Would be my ruin at last.

8. This time tomorrow,
   Reckon where I'll be?
   In some lonesome valley,
   Hangin' on a white oak tree.

147
Trampin'

American Negro Spiritual

Brightly

I'm a - tramp - in', tramp - in', Try-in' to make heav-en my
(Leader in upper notes)
home. (Glo-ry hal-le-lu-jah) Tramp-in', tramp - in', Try-in' to make heav-en my
home. I've nev-er been to heav-en but I've been told,
Verse *Fine* *Leader*
Try-in' to make heav-en my home, The streets up there are
Response *Leader*
paved with gold, Try-in' to make heav-en my home.
Response

2. Sometimes I'm up, sometimes I'm down,
   Tryin' to make heaven my home.
   Sometimes my soul feels heavenly bound,
   Tryin' to make heaven my home.

Continue, as above:

3. See that sister dressed so fine,
   She ain't got religon on her mind.

4. Who's that yonder dressed in blue?
   Must be the children that are comin' through.

5. Who's that yonder dressed in black?
   Must be the hypocrites a-turnin' back.

148
Tumbalalaika

Jewish Folk Song

Moderately fast

Cm   G7

1. Shtet a boch - er und er tracht, Tracht und

Chorus: Tum-ba-la, tum-ba-la, tum-ba-la - lai - ka, — tum-ba-la,

Cm

tracht die gan - tze nacht. Vem-men zu neh - men

tum-ba - la, tum-ba - la - lai - ka. Tum-ba-la - lai - ka,

Fm   Cm   G7   Cm

ohn nit far - schem - men. Vem-men zu neh - men ohn nit far - schem - men.

Shpiel ba - la - lai - ka, Tum-ba - la - lai - ka, Shpiel ba - la - lai - ka.

2. Medel, Medel, 'chvell ba dir fregen,
Vos ken vaksen, vaksen on regen,
Vos ken brennen on nit oifherren,
Vos ken benken, vehnen on trerren.

Chorus

3. Narishe Bocher vos darfst du fregen,
A shtehn ken vaksen, vaksen on regen,
Liebe ken brennen on nit oifherren,
A hartz ken benken, vehnen on trerren.

Chorus

149
The Twelve Days of Christmas

Traditional, English

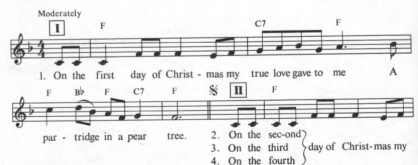

Moderately

I   F   C7   F

1. On the first day of Christ - mas my true love gave to me

A

F   B♭   F   C7   F   𝄋   **II**   F

par - tridge in a pear tree. 2. On the sec-ond
3. On the third ⎬ day of Christ-mas my
4. On the fourth

true love gave to me / two tur-tle doves, / three French hens, / four cal-ling birds, / And a par-tridge in a pear tree.

5. On the fifth day of Christ-mas my true love gave to me

five gold rings, four cal-ling birds, three French hens,

two tur-tle doves, And a par-tridge in a pear tree.

6. On the sixth
7. On the sev-enth
8. On the eighth
9. On the ninth
10. On the tenth
11. On the 'lev-enth
12. On the twelfth
day of Christ-mas my true love gave to me:

Six geese a-lay-ing,
Sev-en swans a-swim-ming,
Eight maids a-milk-ing,
Nine la-dies danc-ing,
Ten lords a-leap-ing,
'Lev-en pip-ers pip-ing,
Twelve drum-mers drum-ming,
five gold rings, four cal-ling birds,

three French hens, two tur-tle doves, And a par-tridge in a pear tree.

149

150
Wanderin'

American Folk Song

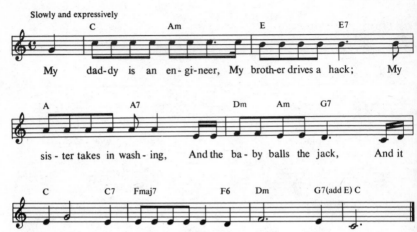

Slowly and expressively

My dad-dy is an en-gi-neer, My broth-er drives a hack; My sis-ter takes in wash-ing, And the ba-by balls the jack, And it looks like I'm nev-er gon-na cease my wan - der-in'.

2. I've been a-wanderin'
   Early and late,
   New York City
   To the Golden Gate,
   An' it looks like
   I'm never gonna cease my wanderin'.

3. Been a-workin' in the army,
   Workin' on a farm,
   All I got to show for it
   Is the muscle in my arm.
   An' it looks like
   I'm never gonna cease my wanderin'.

4. Snakes in the ocean,
   Eels in the sea,
   Red-headed woman
   Made a fool out of me.
   An' it looks like
   I'm never gonna cease my wanderin'.

151
The Water Is Wide

British Folk Song

Moderately

1. Oh, the wa-ter is wide, I can-not cross o - ver,__ And nei-ther
2. A __ ship there__ is and it sails the sea,__ It's load-ed

have I wings to__ fly.____ But give me a boat that
deep as deep can__ be.____ But not so__ deep as this

will car-ry two,____ And both shall row, my love and I.
love I am in,____ I know not how to sink or swim.__

3. I put my hand into the bush
   To pluck a rose of fairest kind.
   The thorns they pierced me at the touch,
   And so I left that rose behind.

4. I leaned my back against an oak.
   I thought it was a trusty tree.
   But first it bended, and then it broke,
   As did my false, false lord to me.

5. Oh, love is sweet and love is fair,
   Fresh as the dew when first it is new,
   But love grows old and waxeth cold,
   And fades away like morning dew.

152

We Three Kings of Orient Are

John H. Hopkins, Jr.   John H. Hopkins, Jr.

Moderately

We three kings of O-ri-ent are; Bear-ing gifts we tra-verse a-far, Field and foun-tain, moor and moun-tain, Fol-low-ing yon-der star. O___ star of won-der, star of night, Star with roy-al beau-ty bright, West-ward lead-ing, still pro-ceed-ing, Guide us to thy per-fect light.

Gaspar:

2. Born a King on Bethlehem's plain,
   Gold I bring to crown him again,
   King forever, ceasing never
   Over us all to reign. (*Chorus*)

Melchior:

3. Frankincense to offer have I,
   Incense owns a Deity nigh;
   Prayer and praising, all men raising,
   Worship Him, God on high. (*Chorus*)

Balthasar:

4. Myrrh is mine: its bitter perfume
   Breathes a life of gathering gloom:
   Sorrowing, sighing, bleeding, dying,
   Sealed in the stone-cold tomb. (*Chorus*)

5. Glorious now behold him arise,
   King and God and sacrifice;
   Alleluia, Alleluia!
   Earth to the heavens replies. (*Chorus*)

153
We Wish You a Merry Christmas

Brightly
(Melody in upper notes)

Traditional English Carol

We wish you a mer-ry Christ-mas, We wish you a mer-ry Christ-mas, We

wish you a mer-ry Christ-mas And a hap - py New Year!   *Fine*

Refrain

Good tid - ings to you, Wher - ev - er you are; Good

tid - ings for Christ-mas And a hap - py New Year!   (We)   *D.C.*

2. Oh, bring us some figgy pudding,
   Oh, bring us some figgy pudding,
   Oh, bring us some figgy pudding,
   With a cup of good cheer.

   Continue, as above:

3. We won't go until we get it, *(3 times)*
   So bring it out here.

4. We all love our figgy pudding *(3 times)*
   With a cup of good cheer.

5. We wish you a merry Christmas *(3 times)*
   And a happy New Year.

153

154
What Child Is This?

William Chatterton Dix

Traditional, English
Arr. by John Stainer

1. What Child is this, Who, laid to rest—On Ma-ry's lap,—is sleep-ing? Whom
2. Why lies he in—such mean es-tate,—Where ox and ass—are feed-ing? Good

an-gels greet with an-thems sweet, While shep-herds watch—are keep-ing?
Chris-tian fear: for sin-ners here—The si-lent Word—is plead-ing.

This, this—is Christ the King, Whom shep-herds guard—and an-gels sing:
Nails, spear, shall pierce him thru,—The Cross be borne,—for me, for you:

Haste, haste—to bring Him laud,—The Babe,—the Son—of Ma-ry!
Hail, hail,—the Word made flesh,—

3. So bring him incense, gold, and myrrh,
    Come, peasant, king, to own him;
The King of kings salvation brings,
    Let loving hearts enthrone him.
Raise, raise the song on high,
    The virgin sings her lullaby:
Joy, joy for Christ is born,
    The babe, the son of Mary!

155
When Johnny Comes Marching Home

Patrick S. Gilmore

Traditional, Irish

Brightly

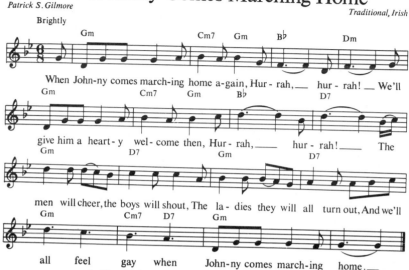

When John-ny comes march-ing home a-gain, Hur - rah, ___ hur - rah! ___ We'll give him a heart-y wel-come then, Hur - rah, ___ hur - rah! ___ The men will cheer, the boys will shout, The la - dies they will all turn out, And we'll all feel gay when John-ny comes march-ing home. ___

2. The old church bell will peal with joy,
   Hurrah, hurrah!
   To welcome home our darling boy,
   Hurrah, hurrah!
   The village lads and lassies say,
   With roses they will strew the way,
   And we'll all feel gay when Johnny comes marching home.

3. Get ready for the Jubilee,
   Hurrah, hurrah!
   We'll give the hero three times three,
   Hurrah, hurrah!
   The laurel wreath is ready now
   To place upon his loyal brow,
   And we'll all feel gay when Johnny comes marching home.

4. Let love and friendship on that day,
   Hurrah, hurrah!
   Their choicest treasures then display,
   Hurrah, hurrah!
   And let each one perform some part,
   To fill with joy the warrior's heart,
   And we'll all feel gay when Johnny comes marching home.

156
When the Saints Go Marching In

American Negro Spiritual

Moderately fast

Lead Voices

Oh, when the saints _____ go march-ing in, _____

Harmony Voices

Oh, when the saints go march-ing

_____ Oh, when the saints go march - ing in. _____

in. saints go march - ing, go march-ing

_____ Lord, how I want to be in that num - ber, _____

in. Oh, let me be in that num-ber, pre-cious

_____ When the saints go march - ing in. _____

num-ber, when the saints go march - ing, go march-ing in.

2. And when the revelation comes,
   And when the revelation comes,
   Lord, how I want to be in that number,
   When the revelation comes.

Continue, as above:

3. And when the new world is revealed.

4. Oh, when they gather 'round the throne.

5. And when they crown him King of kings.

6. And when the sun no more will shine.

7. And when the moon has turned to blood.

8. And on that hallelujah day.

9. And when the earth has turned to fire.

10. Oh, when the saints go marching in.

157
White Coral Bells

Traditional Round

158
Why Shouldn't My Goose ?

Traditional English Round

Why should-n't my goose Sing as well as thy goose,

When I paid for my goose Twice as much as thine?

159
Worried Man Blues

American Folk Song

It takes a wor-ried man to sing a wor-ried song, It

takes a wor-ried man to sing a wor-ried song. It

takes a wor-ried man to sing a wor-ried song, I'm wor-ried

now, _____ But I won't be wor-ried long. _____

2. I went across the river and I lay down to sleep,
   I went across the river and I lay down to sleep,
   I went across the river and I lay down to sleep,
   And I woke up with shackles on my feet.

   Continue, as above:

3. Twenty-one links of chain wrapped around my leg,
   And on each link, an initial of my name.

4. I asked the judge what might be my fine,
   Twenty-one years on the R.C. Mountain Line.

5. Twenty-one long years to pay my awful crime,
   Twenty-one years—but I got ninety-nine.

6. When the train arrived, it was sixteen coaches long,
   The girl I love is on that train and gone.

7. I looked down the track as far as I could see,
   Little bitty hand was waving after me.

8. If anyone should ask you who composed this song,
   Tell them it was I, and I sing it all day long.

160
Zum Gali Gali

Moderately

Israeli Folk Song

2. A-vo-dah le'man he-cha-lutz;
   He-cha-lutz le'man a-vo-dah.

3. He-cha-lutz le'man ha-b'tulah;
   Ha-b'tulah le'man he-cha-lutz.

4. Ha-shalom le'man ha'-amin;
   Ha'-amin le'man ha-shalom.